Black Youth Rising

Black Youth Rising

ACTIVISM AND RADICAL HEALING
IN URBAN AMERICA

Shawn A. Ginwright

TEACHERS COLLEGE PRESS

TEACHERS COLLEGE | COLUMBIA UNIVERSITY

Published by Teachers College Press, 1234 Amsterdam Avenue, New York, NY 10027

Notorious B.I.G. lyrics on p. 7 excerpted from "Things Done Changed," © 1994 Sony/ATV Music Publishing LLC. Written by Owens, Scott, and Wallace. Big Poppa Music (EMI April Music) and EMI April Music (EMI Music Publishing). Rights, in part, administered by Sony/ATV Music Publishing LLC, 8 Music Square West, Nashville, TN 37203. All rights reserved. Rights, in part, to Next Class Music, Brooklyn, NY 11212.

Library of Congress Cataloging-in-Publication Data

Ginwright, Shawn A.
   Black youth rising : activism and radical healing in urban America / Shawn A. Ginwright
        p.   cm.
   Includes bibliographical references and index.
   ISBN 978-0-8077-5021-6 (pbk : alk. paper) — ISBN 978-0-8077-5022-3 (cloth : alk. paper)
   1. African American youth—California—Oakland—Psychology. 2. African American youth—California—Oakland—Attitudes. 3. African American youth—California—Oakland—Conduct of life. 4. Race discrimination—California—Oakland. 5. Community life—California—Oakland. 6. Social justice—California—Oakland. 7. Oakland (Calif.)—Race relations. 8. Oakland (Calif.)—Social conditions. I. Title.

   F869.O2G455   2010
   305.235089'96079466—dc22

                                                                    2009028214

ISBN: 978-0-8077-5021-6 (paper)
ISBN: 978-0-8077-5022-3 (cloth)

Printed on acid-free paper
Manufactured in the United States of America

18   8 7

Contents

Acknowledgments

"Holla back"

WHEN I SET OUT to write this book, I figured that hard work, time to write, and a steadfast commitment to complete the manuscript would be more than enough to produce a meaningful piece of work. I was completely wrong. I realized rather quickly that without friends, family, and colleagues this book would still be incomplete. There are numerous people I would like to thank for support, guidance, feedback, and encouragement to complete this project.

This book would not be possible without the Leadership Excellence family. So much of my thinking about these issues has been shaped, and continues to be shaped, by conversations with the LE community. Daniel Walker, thanks for the vision, my brotha! My dear sista Dereca Blackmon, who took over the helm of the Leadership Excellence ship after my departure, your leadership, commitment to freedom, and sheer genius continues to inspire me. Saleem Shakir, your courageous leadership, bold vision, and dedication to our youth will take Leadership Excellence through its next exciting 20 years of work. Many of the ideas discussed in this book came from debates, conversations, and discussions with my very good friend Macheo Payne. There probably is no other person in the country who knows more about how to reach the hearts and minds of African American youth than brotha Macheo. Thanks, Macheo, for always listening and talking about what is really important. To my comrade and friend Sean Irving: Chinua Achebe said that sometimes "things fall apart" but can always be put back together. Thank you, Sean, for your insight, commitment, and absolute love for our children. The old-school LE crew, Tracy Simmons, Janice Barnes, Dina Walker, Ike Williams, Aisha Bilal, Ginji Perault, sista Adé Mosely, Kisha Grove, Cheryl Jackson, Faith Battles, Vernelle, Greg Hodge, Jumoke Hodge, Kafi Payne, Jason Seals, and brotha Muntu Mbonisi, thanks for always being down for the cause. The new-school LE crew, Adrianne Gillyard, Jasiyah Al-Amin, Jonathan Brumfield, Liz Derias, Mika McGaffie, David Philoxene, and Brenden Anderson, y'all keep the flame for justice going. Randa Powell, what can I say. You are the dream of our work! Because of you, LE lives on and always will.

There are thousands of young people whom I have met throughout my journey with Leadership Excellence. Each of them have left an indelible mark on my heart. Jasmon "Jazzy" Jackson, Tyrone "Philly" Anderson, Iesha Tyler, Ronnel Clayton, Jasmine "J" Braggs, brotha Sid, Tyree Moore, Virgle Laflur, and Cecilia "CC" McClaren: Thanks for your sharing; I have learned so much from each of you.

The ideas in this book are shaped by a number of colleagues and friends. My good friend Julio Cammarota, thanks for your review of earlier drafts of the manuscript and for helping me think of an appropriate title. Thanks to Aleshia "Poole" White for the honest feedback on earlier drafts of the book, and to Isar Godreau at the University of Puerto Rico in Cayey, who provided me the opportunity to teach and complete the manuscript during my stay in Puerto Rico. My friends Antwi Akom, Jeff Duncan Andrade, and Pedro Noguera, thanks for our many "next level" thinking conversations and for strengthening my intellectual muscle to move these ideas forward. Dr. Wade Nobles and Dorothy Tsuruta, thanks for sharpening my ideas about culture and healing.

Thanks to my research assistants, Tina Martin, Janasha Higgins, Anjalee Beverty, and Mike Leveque, who toiled over hours of audio and video tapes. Chiara Cannella, Dorea Kelker, and Sabaa Shoraka, your insights about youth activism and project management of the Research Collaborative on Youth Activism made this book possible. Thanks to Antonia Darder and Rafael Diaz at the Cesar Chavez Institute at San Francisco State University, whose incredible vision for social justice continues to inspire me.

I cannot say thank you enough to my family, who have always supported me, loved me, and believed in me. Mom and Dad (Mae Ginwright and William Ginwright) have always believed in me and encouraged me to dream beyond what I could see. "Little boy with a big ambition, one day gonna hold a high position"; I guess Grandpaw was right. Thanks to my brothers, Graylin and Chris, who are living examples of strong black men. Auntie and Mamma Joyce, your example paved the way for me, and my growth is rooted in your love and support. The Hawkins family, David, Miko, and Justin, y'all, thanks for all your support. Jerry and Ed Logans, and Earl "the Pearl Duke" White, thank you for the gift of your daughter. To my children, Takai and Nyah, "love" is simply an insufficient word to express how much I adore you. You are my life and my inspiration and my dreams. You know that you were born to do good and great things! Nedra, my love and my light: Thank you for being my partner through this journey. Your vision, companionship, and love are my foundation and your grace allows me to soar! I love you.

This book is dedicated to Jerry Logans, Edward Forman, Anna Bowman, and Dr. Henry Wilson. I move confidently in this life knowing that I carry your dreams to make this world a better place.

Introduction

I SIMPLY DID NOT know what to say to these youth. I had brought them up here into these beautiful mountains to pour out their hopes, dreams, and fears, and now nearly all 65 of them (the thugs and the squares) are weeping, looking to me to lead them back to sanity. They wanted me to somehow tell them that what they just heard and witnessed was some type of an illusion and that everything would be all right. But I could not lie to them, nor did I want to, and quite honestly I was in uncharted territory and I did not know what to say to them. I was both emotionally and physically exhausted and the past 5 days had taken a toll on my voice and quite frankly I was at a loss for words.

So we all just sat for a while in this grassy meadow in the warm August sun listening to the birds chirping and to the sounds of the breeze through the trees, hoping that the sobbing and crying would subside. The campus of the University of California, Santa Cruz, feels much more like a summer retreat facility than a college campus. It's not just the large redwood forest, or the fact that you see more deer grazing on campus than students, that gives one this impression. It's the hillside view of the beautiful Pacific Ocean and the sweet fragrance of the sea that puts folks at ease. This is precisely what we needed to reflect on, dialogue about, and heal from the violence in Oakland during the summer of 1998. This year at summer camp on the campus of UC Santa Cruz, the youth shared their souls. They needed to heal from the pain and fear from losing loved ones before they could hope and dream again.

Every year since 1989, I, along with a group of friends, have organized a summer camp for African American youth that we hoped would be a catalyst to reengage black youth into the type of social change America had experienced in the 1960s. By focusing on what black youth do well, and not on their problems, we believed that intense self-exploration and healing from traumatic experiences could awaken in black youth a radical spirit needed to transform their lives, their communities, and ultimately our society. The vision for this summer camp came from African American studies courses I took as a freshman at San Diego State University in 1987, and was an important point in my political consciousness. I never considered myself an activist, despite the fact that both my parents grew up in the segregated South in Jacksonville, Florida, and taught my two brothers and me about southern segregated life. It wasn't until Dr. Shirley Weber challenged us in class to think about how far black America has come since the activism of the 1960s. She would ask us, "Are African Americans better off now than in 1950?" In every class, she inspired us to think about real-life issues in black communities and she pushed us to think about bold solutions and to create self-determined community institutions.

Going to college had been uncomfortably new to me. Not just the information, but attending college on a predominately white campus made me awkwardly self-conscious. In the African American studies faculty offices or in the Black Student Union we could relax and be ourselves. There we did not have to speak for the entire race, as was frequently expected in our classes. Around other black students, we didn't have to worry about pronouncing words perfectly or fear professors and students questioning our intelligence. Perhaps what influenced me most was the community of black students on campus who shared an ideology and spirit for social change and justice. I was awakened to a way of seeing the world as a place of political possibilities.

In 1988, I met Daniel Walker, a dynamic young student, whom I now consider to be one of the most intelligent people I have ever met. His down-to-earth, comedic personality reminds me of a cousin whom you haven't seen in years. It was no surprise that Daniel was perhaps one of the most well-liked people on campus. Even though he was born and raised in Fontana, California, he was a southern boy at heart. His dark skin, short stature, and sharp wit were always accompanied by a hearty laugh or a smile with a signature gap. As 2nd-year students, we were both enrolled in the same African American studies classes. I was always amazed by how he could memorize entire passages from the writings of James Baldwin, Zora Neal Hurston, and Malcolm X that would take me weeks to understand. After about a year, he confessed that he had a photographic memory, something I never knew existed. Similar to my experience, the African American studies courses had profoundly influenced Daniel's political consciousness and commitment to justice in black communities.

Not long after I met Daniel he encouraged me to work with him at a local middle school in San Diego. Together we created a program at the school for "problem students." From 1987 until 1990, our responsibility was to create a class for students whom other teachers found disruptive, inattentive, and sometimes violent. As I reflect on the flexibility the school gave us, I now understand that the school's primary motivation was to keep these students off the streets, out of jail, and alive "by any means necessary." That meant that Daniel and I had extraordinary freedom to design and develop whatever strategy we thought would work. Being young and idealistic, we tried everything, from teaching them black history lessons to outright physical confrontation. We both learned early on that working with youth was more an art than a science. No books could prepare us for the stories and experiences youth would share with us.

On one occasion Michael Barnett (Mike), a lanky 14-year-old student at the school, was kicked out of his history class for disruption. Mike lived near the school and was struggling to avoid involvement in the gang life that had consumed most of his friends. I saw Mike about twice a week for his getting in trouble with one of his teachers. I had been working with him for nearly a year, and I would always chuckle when he would walk into our small office at the school with his hat slightly tilted to the right and with the nonchalant swagger that many young black males use to convey the idea that "I'm not trippin'." I began with the usual series of interrogating questions: "What happened?" "Why did you do this?" "What other choice could you have made?" I liked Mike because he was funny and smart and had a knack of charming his way out of trouble. We developed a sort of big brother/ally relationship, and I took a special interest him because of his leadership on campus. He was the type of teen that other students respected. One day he came into our office and, for some reason, wanted to talk about what it was like to go to "State" (San Diego State University). Surprised and shocked that he had expressed interest in college, I began to describe all the fun aspects of college (parties, football games, girls) just to keep him interested and engaged in the conversation. Secretly, I hoped that his interest in college would ultimately lead him to San Diego State. We talked for nearly an hour and as he left, I was so inspired and excited that I began to immediately call friends and contacts at SDSU to set up a college tour for him and a few other students.

About a week had passed before I began to wonder why Mike had neither come to see me nor been sent to my office. I wanted to talk to him about taking him and a few students to a black fraternity and sorority Step Show on campus. Of course, I had also managed to slip in a meeting with a friend who was an admission counselor, as well as a visit to my favorite African American studies classes. I was certain that the visit to SDSU would encourage Mike to go to college. But when I called his home to provide the details, no one returned my calls. When I saw one of Mike's friends, I told him to ask Mike to come by the office so that I could give him the good news. That's when I learned that Mike had been shot and killed over the weekend.

There are some moments in our lives that change us forever. The news of Mike hit me hard, from the blind side. I felt as though the wind had been knocked out of me. In some ways I have never fully recovered from that blow in 1987. I often hold on to the memory of that experience to remind myself of the importance of the work that I do. No other experience has influenced my thinking about the needs of black youth more than the loss of Mike at what was probably a turning point in his life. What could I had done differently? Should I have taken him to campus as soon as I met him? Could I have saved his life? These questions both haunt me but also motivate me to search for new ways to engage Black youth.

After Mike's death, I began intense questioning about my life and began to doubt that simply attaining a college education would be enough for confronting the crisis in urban America. During this time, black college students around the country began to embrace nationalistic symbols and icons. We wore Malcolm X T-shirts and listened to positive hip-hop from groups like X-Clan, Public Enemy, and A Tribe Called Quest. No outfit was complete without a red, black, and green "X" medallion, which to me signified an emerging political consciousness. In 1989, Spike Lee released the movie *Do the Right Thing*, which highlighted the racial tensions and unresolved questions about the post–civil rights United States. The film, and his visit to the San Diego State University campus to debut the movie, made conversations about race, racism, and activism irresistible. Perhaps this energy led black students on campus to be more involved in the antiapartheid movement where we protested the University of California's investments in the oppressive South African economy.

The political ideology from African American studies, the explosion of black nationalistic images in popular culture, and the energy surrounding the antiapartheid movement, however, did not address the unprecedented number of black male homicide victims in black urban America. Mike's death, unfortunately, was not an anomaly. In fact, thousands of black youth in urban cities throughout the United States experienced unprecedented violence and homicides. In Los Angeles County in 1989 there were numerous homicide victims, most of which were of black youth between the ages of 14 and 25. Similar trends occurred in New York, Chicago, Oakland, and San Diego.

In the decade between 1988 and 1998, black families in urban America experienced the loss of thousands of youth to violence. In San Diego, the unemployment rate had soared to 11.3% for blacks, leaving hundreds of young black males searching for income. The introduction of crack cocaine, combined with the lack of job opportunities, funneled numerous black youth into the drug economy. In just 6 years, the number of San Diego's homicide victims went from 96 in 1985 to 167 by 1991 (City of San Diego, 2007). This trend was not unique to San Diego. Similar trends were occurring in urban cities throughout the United States (see Figure I.1). Nationally, the homicide victimization rate for black males between the ages of 18 and 24 in 1985 was 73.3% (Fox & Zawitz, 2007).

Figure I.1. U.S. homicide victimization r ates among black and white males aged 18–24, 1985–2005.

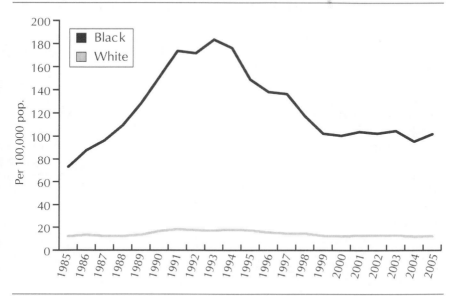

Source: Fox & Zawitz, 2007.

By 1993, the rate had dramatically jumped to 183.5% (Fox & Zawitz, 2007). In response to the dramatic increase in the homicide rate, the term "black youth" became synonymous with "predator" in the minds of the general public (Males, 1996, 1999). Ideas such as the "war on drugs" and the "war on crime" ushered in a public assault on black youth and their communities. Mike Males (1999) documented how xenophobic notions of youth as well as fear of crime helped to shape public policy hostile to African American youth during the 1990s. Legislators responded by crafting public policy that underscored the idea that to be black, young, and poor was also to be criminal (Males & Macallair, 2000). These negative perceptions were reinforced through public policies that increased repression through institutions such as schools, law enforcement, and the juvenile justice system (Butts, 1999). From 1994 to 2000, for example, 43 states instituted legislation that facilitated the transfer of children to adult court. The result of these laws was to dismantle a long-standing belief that special protections and rehabilitation were necessary to protect youth from the effects of the adult justice system. As a result, in 1996 African American youth were 6 times more likely to be incarcerated and received longer sentences than their white counterparts in Los Angeles County. When charged with the same violent crime, blacks were 9 times more likely to be sentenced; for drug offenses they were sent to prison 48 times more often than whites charged with the same crimes (Poe-Yamagata & Jones, 2000). These profound constraints on life opportunities over time take a toll on hope, aspirations, and political possibilities.

THINGS DONE CHANGED: POSTCRACK BLACK URBAN AMERICA

Mike's death and the profound regularity of losing other youth to violence in San Diego forced me to question my own activism. I had doubts that lessons from the civil rights movement strategies that we learned about in class could confront the crisis among black youth in urban America. To me ending "black-on-black violence," as the media labeled the phenomenon, seemed to be a different type of political aim from that of the civil rights movement or black power movement.

Daniel and I struggled to make sense of Mike's death and often debated the complex issues facing black communities. Our debates would often end with his laughing at me because I couldn't substantiate my argument. "You see Shawn, you gotta reread *Wretched of the Earth*; Fanon lays it out right in front of us!" In an effort to be better armed for our next intellectual encounter, I would visit the library and skim the book or article that he referenced. One time, however, as I reviewed Franz Fanon's *Wretched of the Earth*, I was intrigued by how Fanon discussed the psychological impact of colonialization on Africans. Not only was his study of Algeria an examination of the colonial impact on African identity and culture, but also he forced me to think about the similar colonial impact of white domination on black culture.

The internal oppression (shame and hatred of blackness) created by external marginalization (colonialism, structural racism, and poverty) seemed to me a powerful explanation of the rise of black youth violence in urban America. The concept of internalized oppression also allowed me to understand Mike's untimely death as a result of both a failed public policy and a growing sense of internalized oppression and fatalism among black youth. Recalling Fanon's notion of internalized oppression among blacks in Algeria, black youth in San Diego and other urban cities internalized the rage from structural racism and directed their hate toward each other.

Mike had got into an altercation with three young men at the local skating rink. His friends said that Mike was approached in the bathroom by three young men who attempted to take his gold necklace. The on-duty security guard stopped the scuffle and as Mike was leaving he commented to his assailants, "Y'all niggas ain't shit." When he returned home, the same three young men decided to shoot him as he exited the bus that stopped directly across from the apartment complex where he lived. They didn't even know Mike.

Something had fundamentally changed not only in black communities, but also in our spirit. The sense of fatalism, hopelessness, and rage had redefined black community life, particularly among black youth. By 1997, Notorious B.I.G had perhaps most poignantly articulated what many of us secretly knew, which was that the widespread violence was rupturing the fabric of the black community:

> Back in the days, our parents used to take care of us
> Look at em now, they even fuckin scared of us
> Callin the city for help because they can't maintain
> Damn, shit done changed . . .[1]

At the time, I could not identify, or explain, the structural transformation in the economy that formed what Wilson (1996) called the "black underclass." All I knew was that something had fundamentally changed in black community life, and it was killing thousands of black youth. Daniel and I concluded that activism in the post–civil rights era had to deal with both the dismantling of structural barriers to opportunities, and the internal consequences of exposure to years of intensified urban poverty. More than electoral politics, community organizing, and advocating for better public policy, we concluded that activism in the post–civil rights era should rebuild hope and heal communities from the trauma of urban violence and racial marginalization. We didn't render electoral politics, community organizing, and civil rights strategies obsolete, but rather, we believed that healing and hope were critical prerequisites for activism and social change.

BUILDING A NEW TYPE OF COMMUNITY ORGANIZATION

It was with an understanding of the political importance of healing and hope that Daniel and I embarked upon the journey to create an organization that would confront the crisis facing African American youth. We wanted it to combat internalized oppression and build the skills African American youth needed to address community problems. With no money, no bank account, and only an idea, we launched a summer camp that would capture the imagination, hopes, dreams, and fears of African American youth. We called on black fraternities and sororities, African American studies majors, and black student groups to serve as counselors at the first camp, which was held in July 1989. We recruited about 20 college student counselors and trained them in what we believed to be our mission and philosophy at the time and rolled with it. The first camp was held on the campus of San Diego State University and drew nearly 50 high school students from three high schools in San Diego.

We did not really know at the time that what would transpire over those 4 days at the camp would alter the direction of our lives. Looking back, we probably were not ready for what we witnessed at that first camp. The stories young people shared about their hopes and dreams, loss and trauma exceeded our expectations. Perhaps what I remember most about that first camp was the feeling that we had built something that young people had been waiting for. It recalled that scene in the movie *Field of Dreams*—"If you build it, they will come." Young people talked openly about guilt from committing acts of violence; they talked about wanting to go to college; they shared the excitement of shooting a gun and the guilt that came from knowing their bullet took a life. Most important, however, we learned that youth wanted to talk about things that had been on their minds and hearts for some time.

Nearly 20 years later, our organization, called Leadership Excellence, has worked with more than 10,000 African American young people in California. The strategy we have used is simple: build a strong caring relationship, nurture healthy racial identities among African American youth, and foster a strong political consciousness about community issues in ways that compel them to confront pressing neighborhood problems. These practices constitute more than a strategy to engage youth in civic affairs. Rather, this strategy constitutes what I have called "radical healing," building the capacity of young people to act upon their environment in ways that contribute to the common good. This process contributes to individual well-being, community health, and broader social justice, whereby young people can act on the behalf of others with hope, joy, and a sense of possibility.

Healing occurs in everyday life when black youth confront racial profiling in their neighborhoods, fight for free bus passes to get to school, demand access to bathrooms that work in their schools, and present impromptu theater on street corners to inspire youth to vote. These acts require a consciousness of possibilities and are fostered through strong, caring relationships and spaces that encourage black youth to see beyond present-day community conditions. When black youth are conscious of the root causes of the problems they face, they act in profound ways to resist and transform issues they view as unjust.

This requires that we conceptualize oppression as a form of social and collective trauma. This view of oppression allows us to identify and name the cultural, social, and spiritual consequences of trauma for oppressed communities. Trauma conveys the idea that oppression and injustice inflict harm. Effectively responding to oppression, therefore, requires a process that restores individuals and communities to a state of well-being. Radical healing points to the process of building hope, optimism, and vision to create justice in the midst of oppression.

Healing from the trauma of oppression caused by poverty, racism, sexism, homophobia, and class exploitation is an important political act. Without a critical understanding of how the various structures of domination operate in our daily lives we cannot begin to develop meaningful forms of personal and collective resistance. Daily trauma, hopelessness, and nihilism "prevent us from participating in organized collective struggle aimed at ending domination and transforming society" (hooks, 1993, p. 15). Healing occurs when we reconcile painful experiences resulting from oppression through testimony and naming what may seem to be personal misfortune as systemic oppression.

Understanding the personal and political dimensions of daily life, however, requires a critical consciousness, a way of understanding the social world through political resistance and freedom. This notion of resistance occurs in communities where the capacity to confront racism and other forms of domination teach youth what they need to know about the world and how to change things in it (Ward, 2000). Ward suggests that these communities are intimate spaces where young people "cultivate resistance against beliefs, attitudes, and practices that can erode a Black child's self-confidence and impair her positive identity development" (p. 51). The power to speak about painful experiences related to racism, sexism, and poverty facilitates healing because the act of testifying exposes the raw truth about suffering and releases the hidden pain that is a profound barrier to resistance.

Healing as a form of political resistance is not a phenomenon new to black life. In fact, spirituals, drumming, the blues, sermons, and of course the black church have served as important outlets for testifying about personal and collective trauma and also receiving support in a loving community. For example, enslaved Africans used these spaces for healing and sharing, even though the spaces were under constant attack. When the drum was prohibited, spoken word emerged in its place to defend and sustain these healing spaces. Healing, in this sense, has always served an important function in black political and social life.

Four areas of black life contribute to the radical healing process. First, caring relationships connect people in profound ways to meaningful acts of resistance. *Caring relationships* in this sense does not imply simply individual acts of kindness; rather, care prepares black youth to know themselves as part of a long history of struggle and triumph. Second, radical healing occurs in *community* where the space to imagine and hope encourage young people to shed their fear and pain in order to move forward with love and optimism. Third, developing a critical *consciousness* about their social world prepares black youth to resist various forms of oppression. This form of consciousness focuses on building an awareness of the intersections of personal and political life by pushing youth to understand how personal struggles have profound political explanations. Finally, *culture* serves as an anchor to connect young people to a racial and ethnic identity that is both historically grounded and contemporarily relevant. This view of culture both embraces the importance of a healthy African identity for black youth and celebrates the vibrancy and ingenuity of urban black youth culture.

BUILDING SPACES FOR RADICAL HEALING

Radical healing is rooted in vibrant community life where love, hope, and goodness outweigh problems. However, we have to remember and sometimes envision these communities in order to resurrect them. Not long ago, I had a conversation with some close friends about growing up in black urban America during the 1970s. Our stories were nostalgic descriptions of common experiences black folks shared growing up poor in urban areas. Just about every story would be filled with heartfelt humor and a sense of longing for the ways that we navigated, engaged, and participated in urban life as children and youth. The remarkable common experiences that we shared invoked in me a curiosity about not so much what happened to the "good ole days in the hood," but rather what has remained. Sharing stories like, "Do y'all remember your momma telling you to come home with the streetlights came on?" Or the numerous stories about the ice cream truck that would come up and down our street like clockwork.

Remembering stories is fun, joyful, and hopeful and brings people together in remarkable ways. Stories about running through the water from fire hydrants on hot summer days, playing football on asphalt streets, braiding your friend's hair on the steps of the porch, playing double Dutch after school, or recalling the first time you used a hot comb to press your hair serve as important cultural memories for a generation of adults who, as youth, embraced urban life in ways that define their identity today. When we share these stories, we form the type of community bell hooks (1995) refers to as "beloved community—where loving ties of care and knowing bind us together in our differences," and our collective consciousness builds space where the possibility of remembering, healing, and growing occurs. These stories and the collective cultural memory of urban life "back in the day" allow us to more deeply identify with one another, despite our various differences, and form mutual ties and healing spaces. By sharing these stories, we weave together a tapestry of urban ethnic richness and nuanced communal possibilities that make us laugh, cry, remember, and ultimately hope—all of which form the fabric of a beloved community. It is within these spaces where black youth can envision new possibilities for their lives and their communities.

Communities can provide important healing opportunities— opportunities for youth to reflect, to develop critical consciousness, to hope and to change social conditions. Beyond simply reflecting on the good ole days, conversations in the community invoke what Robin Kelly (2002) has called "radical imagination," which is the revolutionary potential of hope. Kelly suggests that everyday life, and oppressive conditions in urban America, particularly for black youth, render imagination and hope inert. Daily survival and ongoing crisis management in young people's lives make it difficult to see beyond the present. In healing communities, however, battle scars are mended, racial wounds are healed, and ruptured communities are made whole again. Ultimately hope is restored.

Hope and radical imagination are important prerequisites for activism and social change. Together hope and imagination inspire youth to understand that community conditions are not permanent and that the first step to change is imagining new possibilities. Kelly reminds us that hope and imagination may be "the most revolutionary ideas available to us, and yet as intellectuals we have failed miserably to grapple with these political and analytical importance" (2002, pp. 11–12).

Healing involves reconciling the past to change the present while imagining a new future. Invoking the West African term *Sankofa*, I used healing to describe the process of learning from the past in order to move forward. Radical healing is much broader than simply moving from pathology to wellness. The concept focuses on how hope, imagination, and care transform the capacity of communities to confront community problems. For young people, healing fosters a collective optimism and a transformation of spirit that, over time, contributes to healthy, vibrant community life.

Educational, social movement, and youth development research has not adequately addressed the theoretical significance of suffering or considered the empirical dimensions of healing, hope, and freedom. Despite the plethora of research that has documented the ways in which poor black communities collectively experience gentrification, violence, job loss, family dislocation, and substance abuse, few have explored the collective healing process. Long-term exposure to economic abuse, structural violence, and social marginalization has threatened aspects of civic life and community well-being. This is not so much the basis of a deficit model, but more precisely a broader perspective that highlights how over time economic, cultural, and social marginalization can rupture the psychosocial fabric that forms communities of care and fosters collective and individual well-being and purpose. These ingredients are critical to supporting political action.

Radical healing involves building the capacity of young people to act upon their environment in order to create the type of communities in which they want to live. By integrating issues of power, history, self-identity, and the possibility of collective agency and struggle, radical healing rebuilds communities, to foster hope and political possibilities for young people. This process acknowledges the ways in which joblessness, poverty, violence, and poor education have been toxic to black communities. At the same time the process fosters new forms of political and community life. By rebuilding collective identities (racial, gendered, youth), exposing youth to critical thinking about social conditions, and building activism, black youth heal by removing self-blame and act to confront pressing school and community problems.

I have watched the radical healing process occur for hundreds of African American youth in Oakland. It was the radical healing process that created the safety, trust, and hope that allowed all 65 of these youth to openly cry at our summer camp in 1998. For more than an hour, we listened to stories of traumatic events, disappointments, and loss. The breaking point was when a young man shared with the group that he was responsible for a fatal shooting in which he never wanted to participate. He shared with us in vivid detail the haunting night when he experienced the horror of taking a life. He had never shared this with anyone, so he had held this pain and stuffed it away, deep down. After his powerful testimony to the group, he released all that he had been holding in and wept and expressed remorse. Everyone began to cry, not only from his pain, but also from their own unspoken stories. While I didn't know exactly what to say, I knew that our community was healing and being made whole again.

My purpose in writing this book was to create a new dialogue regarding what constitutes activism among black youth in the post–civil rights United States. The central argument throughout the book is that intensified oppression in urban communities has threatened the type of community spaces that foster hope and a political imagination for black youth. These spaces are critical preconditions for collective action because they allow young people to envision the type of communities they want to create. This book examines how despite community conditions, black youth can take action in their communities in ways that contribute to civic life.

Dramatic educational, economic, political, and cultural transformations in urban America, coupled with decades of unmitigated violence, has shaped both constraints and opportunities for activism among black youth. On the one hand, these political and economic forces constrained the form and content of protest activism among black youth. Yet on the other hand, the same forces fostered a form of activism that focuses on building caring relationships, reviving community life, and embracing culture. Sustaining these new forms of activism requires healing, which is a dramatic departure from the radical identity politics of the 1960s and 1970s. Rather than electoral politics, collective action among black youth is directed at less formal aspects of civic life, such as attending neighborhood hip-hop shows and concerts, exchanging information about jobs at the local barbershop, or congregating on the street corner to connect with friends. Through ethnography, this book examines the embodied nature of collective trauma and explores the development of political consciousness and activism among African American youth in a community-based organization in Oakland, California. Four questions shape this book: (1) What constitutes activism among black youth in postcrack urban America? (2) What role do community-based organizations play in fostering activism and well-being among black youth? (3) How can the hopes, aspirations, imagination, and dreams that black youth hold for themselves, their family, and their communities contribute to healing? and (4) How does healing contribute to resistance in school and neighborhood change?

THEORETICAL BACKDROP

In their classic study of black Chicago, St. Clair Drake and Horace Cayton (1993) commented on the relationship between neighborhood decline and the emergence of a perception of "wild children" in Bronzeville. They remarked that Bronzeville's "wild children" were not so numerous as the frightened upper and middle class thought, but there were enough of them roaming the streets during the Depression, stealing, fighting, and molesting pedestrians, to cause everyone—including lower-class parents—to talk about the "youth problem." Today, talk about the "black youth problem" in public policy circles and the general public has also influenced ethnographic research in black communities. In recent years, social science research about black youth has almost entirely focused on understanding various causes of problem behavior, such as violence, school failure, substance abuse, and crime (Anderson, 1990, 1999; Wilson, 1987). While a deeper understanding of these social problems are indeed important, the narrow focus on problems obscures the complex ways in which black youth respond to, challenge, and change conditions in their schools and communities.[2]

Perhaps Wilson's (1996) well-known study on the persistence of black poverty is emblematic of this genre of social science research. Wilson argued that structural changes in the economy shape choices, attitudes, and behaviors among the urban poor and ultimately lead to social disintegration, the eroding of community and family values, and ultimately behaviors that create and sustain poverty. Black youth in urban communities adopt behaviors, values, and attitudes that are barriers to educational achievement, economic mobility, and civic participation. Building from this premise, Elijah Anderson's (1999) ethnography of black families in Philadelphia details how rules, norms, and values unique to urban poverty foster violence and other problematic behaviors among "street" families, while "decent" families struggle to maintain mainstream values, beliefs, and behaviors. Anderson's view of violent and high-risk behavior, particularly related to youth, is viewed as a function of local beliefs and values that are adaptations to economic deprivation. The classification of "street" and "decent" families conveys the notion that middle-class values among "decent" families can mitigate urban violence. Violence became an accepted code of conduct for black youth in this neighborhood. For some, participating in violence earned them respect among their peers, while for others it was a way to navigate risky confrontations on the streets.

Similar conclusions are made about the role of social networks in black youth. Mercer Sullivan draws similar conclusions about the relationship between crime, economic despair, and social organization. He argues that the "distinctive crime patterns of the Projectville group derived not only from the ecological and demographic characteristics but also from the social organization of their environment" (1989, p. 150). Sullivan claims that black youth—unlike white youth, who benefit from strong social networks that connect them to jobs—lack social capital and turn to crime and illegal activities to earn money. Thus, criminal behavior among black youth appears to be the only way that they respond to economic oppression.

While these studies provide an important theoretical frame for understanding the complexity of young people's lives, the underlying thesis is that black youth behaviors can be understood as maladaptive responses to limited economic opportunities in black urban communities.[3] As a result, the empirical study of problems, prevention, and pathology is woven into the theoretical fabric of each of these perspectives. This is particularly the case for research on African American youth in which numerous studies have attempted to explain or show the causes contributing to elevated drug use, high school drop-out rates, violence, early sexual activity, and other behaviors that jeopardize healthy development.[4]

I depart from these researchers' tendency to conceptualize behavior through the social disintegration thesis, which explains youth crime, delinquency, and violence as either individual pathological behavior (Ayman-Nolley & Taira, 2000) or cultural adaptations that stem from social disorganization in communities (Anderson, 1999). Rather, I borrow from the works of Janelle Dance (2002), Joyce West Stevens (2002), and Janie Ward (1995, 2000), who acknowledge the constraints of urban poverty and structural marginalization, but also create space to better understand how black youth navigate through, develop meaning about, and resist social marginalization. Dance accurately comments on what she calls, the "scholarly gaze on black life":

> In clarifying the structural factors that lie beyond the control of individual Black Americans, these sociologists unwittingly suggest that Blacks are *controlled* by these forces, when they mean to convey that Blacks are *constrained*, sometimes severely, by structural forces. (2002, p. 27).

This perspective leaves greater room for agency or the capacity for people to act and respond to sociocultural forces in ways that contribute collective well-being. This approach examines assets in neighborhoods and families and how institutions support youth as they confront daily problems. Additionally, this approach provides us with an opportunity to conceptualize the conditions that threaten community life as well as understand the process that contributes to civic well-being.

The conditions that threaten vibrant community life in urban communities have become increasingly "toxic" to civic well-being. Postindustrial restructuring of urban economies has resulted in high rates of unemployment, a paucity of decent-paying jobs, and the elimination of viable educational opportunities (Wilson, 1987) all of which constrain civic life among urban youth. James Garbarino argues that the presence of violence and poverty in urban communities generates "social toxins . . . a term used to represent the degree to which the social world has become poisonous to a person's well being" (1995, p. 61). Drawing from environmentalists who have identified environmental toxins such as lead paint found in older homes and buildings, pesticides in our soil, or poor air quality from local refineries, Garbarino identifies social equivalents to physical toxins. These might include violence, poverty, domestic and sexual abuse, family disruption, and racism. Youth in poor communities are often most vulnerable to the presence of these toxins, and just as physical toxins can reach dangerous levels, social toxins can severely constrain people's capacity to act (Garbarino, 1995). Symptoms of high levels of social toxicity might include depression, despair, hopelessness, fear, anger, and pain. For youth in black communities, toxicity manifests itself through apathy, fatalism, and self-destructive behaviors (Poussaint & Alexander, 2000).

Understanding social toxins in community settings shifts our focus from solely describing youth behaviors to explaining the conditions in which young people live. Youth behaviors, values, and beliefs are often a rational response to irrational, and often toxic, social, economic, and political conditions (Sánchez-Jankowski, 2008). This perspective forces us to examine more closely the ways in which young people navigate and respond to socially toxic environments in ways that sustain community life. Behavior from this perspective is not simply pathological or prosocial, but rather "probable," given the toxic context in which behavior occurs. Probable behavior is not overly deterministic, because it leaves room for agency and highlights the various choices that young people make in their social settings. Social science has been restricted to conceptualizing behavior in poor neighborhoods through rigid and competing value orientations that view actions as "responsible" or "irresponsible" (Sánchez-Jankowski, 2008). Probable behavior frees us from this debate because it opens theoretical possibilities to understanding the conditions under which young people make choices that contribute to community life.

Despite the constraints on the choices young people make in toxic communities, there are ways in which young people can "detoxify" their social environments. Social detoxification involves removing or neutralizing harmful elements in a social setting. Creating safe neighborhoods in which there was once gun violence and creating jobs and training residents to work are both examples of the social detoxification process. Radical healing is parallel to this process in the social world. It involves preparing young people to confront pressing community problems and shift from individual blame to a consciousness of root and systemic causes of personal problems. This consciousness strengthens individual and collective agency, encourages action that addresses real community problems, and builds an awareness of a common good.

Community organizations can play an important role in healing and responding to neighborhood and community problems (Ginwright, 2007). Often these organizations provide opportunities for urban youth to connect with peers, adults, and experiences that address pressing social and community problems. Sampson (2001) argues that social capital for poor communities must be understood as closely linked to collective efficacy and calls for "the linkage of mutual trust and the shared willingness to intervene for the common good" (p. 95). Sampson, Morenoff, and Earls (1999) argue that "collective efficacy for children is produced by the shared beliefs and a collectively in its conjoint capability for action. The notion of collective efficacy emphasizes residents' sense of active engagement" (p. 635). This perspective allows for defining the purpose of social relationships through actions promoting justice within neighborhoods, churches, and youth programs in low-income urban communities, all of which serve as vital sources for the understanding of civic life for African American youth and their communities.

In many ways, civic organizations are pathways for youth to engage in healing, or what Freire (1993) calls "praxis"—critical reflection and action. Often community-based organizations facilitate the healing process because they foster important relationships and develop critical consciousness necessary for activism (Ginwright, 2007; Ginwright, Noguera, & Cammarota, 2006). Employing Freire's conceptualization of "critical consciousness," I use the term to convey how an awareness of the systematic forms of oppression builds the capacity for self-determination to take action to address social and community problems. Critical consciousness allows youth to see and act differently in the world as agents rather than victims. This notion marks a significant departure from the standard social capital literature, which often fails to recognize both individual and collective agency or how social networks ultimately foster critical consciousness.

Critical consciousness and action promote self-determination and compel individuals and collectives to claim power and control over sometimes daunting social conditions. Power and control over life situations are key for social justice and wellness (Prilleltensky, 2008; Prilleltensky, Nelson, & Pierson, 2001). Wellness encompasses more than striving for the absence of risks and the elimination of community problems. Rather, it points to what individuals need to effectively engage in collective action. Wellness and social justice illustrate that young people's aspirations to create good schools, safe neighborhoods, and a vibrant community life require both individual and collective development.

The relationship between social justice and wellness is an important aspect of radical healing. The capacity to act to improve the quality of life for oneself and others highlights the convergence of both the personal and political dimensions of civic life. Individuals seek power and control both at the personal level, through their own decision making, and at the political level, by organizing their neighborhood to influence public policy. This is precisely the process of liberation that overcomes internal and external sources of oppression. Liberation is both "freedom from" internal and external forms of oppression and "freedom to" pursue dreams, wellness, peace, and a better quality of life (Prilleltensky, 2008). This pursuit of justice and freedom, in this sense, yields both internal capacity to resist domination as well as builds social capital and a greater external capacity to act to create better community conditions.

Wellness is a result of power and control over internal and external forms of oppression (Prilleltensky et al., 2001; Watts & Guessous, 2006). Radical healing facilitates wellness on three levels (Figure I.2). First, individual-level wellness focuses on strengthening political and social consciousness, hope, optimism, and voice among young people. Particularly important is building the critical consciousness necessary to resist domination and create a better way of life. Often social justice researchers, educators, and practitioners focus almost entirely on youth resistance without conceptualizing the critical importance of creating. For young people, individual wellness provides an internal capacity and resilience to engage in civic and social justice efforts. Second, community-level wellness focuses on collective power and control over local public policy. As young people heal, they also form communities where a collective consciousness drives people to act to achieve social justice. Community wellness involves community organizing, planning a neighborhood block party, or attending a public hearing about a school closure. These examples of community wellness signal trust, relationships, networks, and optimism about the capacity for social change. Third, through social-level wellness, young people engage in social movements and other forms of collective action. Robust and healthy democratic life requires debate, contestation, and participation, all of which signal social well-being.

An eclectic grouping of ideas from African American literature, readings in African-centered psychology, and community psychology research also shapes this book. Feeling restricted by the confines of social science research to capture the nuances and textured realities of urban life among black youth, I have attempted to weave together a set of ideas that highlight the joy, beauty, and strengths of black youth. These ideas are held together by the belief that black urban life is not simply suffering, survival, and struggle and that despite historic and contemporary racial oppression, justice, hope, and imagination are present in black life. These ideas largely come from James Baldwin's passionate and eloquent writing on black life, dignity, and justice. Baldwin, as a novelist and artist who was unrestricted by disciplinary boundaries, had at his disposal a rich kaleidoscope of colors and textures to describe the nuanced experience of what it means to be black in the United States. I use Baldwin's essays, as well as key concepts from cultural studies critiques, such as those by Audry Lourde, bell hooks, and Robin Kelly, to convey the fluid nature of black youth culture and the ways in which power is constantly negotiated and contested in urban America.

Figure I.2. Radical healing model.

Urban Conditions ⇧	Urban Social Toxins ⇧	Radical Healing ⇧	Wellness
Exodus of jobs	Interpersonal Violence Fear Shame Uncertainty Nihilism Loss of control	Care Agency Hope and optimism Resistance Personal transformation Struggle against racism, sexism, homophobia, classism Political and social awareness	Social Social movements Collective action Liberation Freedom "from" oppression Freedom "to" create Social justice Peace
Emerging crack cocaine economy	Structural Poverty Family dislocation Lack of access to health care Racism Poor-quality schools	Community Solidarity	Community Community solidarity Collective consciousness Community power, civic action Relationships, trust, social capital Community thriving
Decline of black radicalism		Consciousness	Individual Political and social consciousness Hope and optimism Voice Freedom to create Resistance
Historical and contemporary racism		Culture	

Power and Control

Community and Civic Action

JAZZ AND A NOTE ON METHODOLOGY

In order to highlight both the aesthetic and empirical aspects of this study, I used aspects of jazz music to frame my methodology. I have always loved jazz music. I remember my father would stretch out on the brown shag carpet in our house and, after a hard day's work, would plug in his puffy black earphones into the hi-fi system in our living room to escape, relax, and perhaps dream through jazz music. I would lie on his chest, and he would place the headphone over my ears, so that I could share moments of his dreaming with him. He explained to me that jazz was like telling a beautiful story. Each member of the band, at precisely the right time, would retell the story, all giving their own interpretation, sometimes only highlighting their favorite parts of the story, other times adding something entirely new, somehow keeping the essence of the story intact, unchanged and beautiful. He would flip through the stack of albums and, with anticipation, I would wait for him to place the needle on the record. After a few cracks, "On Green Dolphin Street" would always put me to sleep. I did not know at the time that he was listening to John Coltrane, Miles Davis, and Cannonball Adderley, but somehow, the notes, rhythms, and sounds made an indelible mark upon my appreciation of the art form.

It wasn't until college that I really began to understand the technology and the art of jazz. Turns out, my roommate was a jazz pianist. He would listen to jazz for hours in our cramped studio apartment. "Jazz is about improvisation," he would explain; "it's about always pushing the limits of the art form without disrespecting it." But there is something about jazz that is more than technique and skill. For me, the music both informs and inspires and brings together the confluence of art and science. The notion of bringing together art and science poses an interesting challenge for those of us who study and advocate for youth. Namely, in what ways does our work move beyond simplistic explanations, descriptions, and predictions of youth behaviors? How can our work both inform and inspire?

My ideas about jazz and methodology stem from Sara Lawrence-Lightfoot's notion of portraiture, which "pushes against the constraints of those traditions and practices in its explicit effort to combine empirical and aesthetic descriptions" of people's lives in context (1997, p. 13). The approach pays particular attention to the ways in which "goodness" rather than pathology is practiced in everyday life. Studying what is good about black youth, rather than only describing problems, requires relentless attention to empirical description and aesthetic expression. How can the aesthetic aspects of jazz—the bass line, syncopation, and improvisation—give meaning to the empirical structure of ethnographic inquiry?

To answer this question, I use elements of jazz music to frame my observations and interpret my descriptions of social settings. Jazz is often marked by a bass line that gives structure to the boundaries, form, tempo, and cadence of pulsating harmonic accents all woven together by melodic themes. Notes dance in and out of time and collide into perfect harmony and syncopation to tell a simple and beautiful story. First, my methods involved "bass line" observations, which are detailed and solid descriptions of neighborhoods, landmarks, and other social settings. The reverberation of the bass is given meaning through solid community descriptions, sound historical observations, and thick renderings of social settings. Second, I used harmonic observations, which focus on social interactions within particular settings. Harmonic observations highlight what people do, how they do it, and why they are doing it and adds meaning to bass-line observations. Weaving in and around the bass line, harmonic observations provide personal stories and add texture, color, and meaning to the triumphs and struggles in young people's lives. Last, I used melodic observations, which are perhaps the most aesthetic aspect of my methods. Melodic observations highlight the nuances in people's expressions and subtleties in voice and style of dress, which provide poignant staccato insights into young people's personalities. Melodic observations give detailed descriptions and are meant to blend timbre and unique voicing and add fine details to the study.

My medium, however, is not sound, it is text. Good scientific work, then, just as in jazz, should both inform and inspire, and in its doing so, we pose new questions, challenge assumptions, and ultimately move together in an entirely different direction. In the same spirit of jazz, there is an improvisational nature to this work as well. After hours of observing young people, I would bounce ideas back and forth with them and discuss the meaning of what I had observed. After several discussions, I would return to my observations until I developed a melody that I could explain—a theory, so to speak.

The melody came from 15 years of working with urban youth who participated in Leadership Excellence, as noted earlier, located in Oakland, California. After years of rich insights, I wanted to describe the strengths and collective assets among black youth and better understand how young people collectively respond to neighborhood problems to improve conditions for their families, schools, and communities. For nearly 5 years, I observed and documented through extensive field notes the educational and organizational processes and practices that promote youth healing and agency.

The data for this book were collected over a 5-year period (2000–2005) and largely consisted of participant observation and interviews of 10 African American youth from Leadership Excellence. My observations occurred largely during the organization's summer events, such as summer camps, and during weekly political education meetings. These observations also extended into their schools, local shopping centers, and occasionally homes. My process involved collecting extensive field notes of observations of group meetings at the summer program, conversations as they traveled to other parts of the city, and one-on-one informal conversations. There were generally two types of observations: descriptions of what I had witnessed or heard and details of what I found interesting or surprising.

During my participation and observations in many of the meetings, discussions, and summer programs, I was not a distant, objective observer. In fact, I often facilitated many of the group sessions, and as the founder/ director, I also designed many of the programs and pedagogical strategies. I am also a longtime resident of Oakland and have a rather wide social network of individuals, families, and institutions that all have, at one time or another, worked with me on issues to improve the quality of life for Oakland's youth. As a result, numerous informal conversations with public officials, teachers, school board members, youth workers, and community residents about life in Oakland influenced this study.

ORGANIZATION OF THE BOOK

Chapter 1 introduces the reader to Oakland through a bus ride down International Boulevard, Oakland's main street. This ethnographic account of the city provides the reader with a geopolitical understanding of Oakland. The chapter also sets the context for understanding why healing has important political significance for black youth in urban communities. Through the story of 66-year-old Roland and his 20-year-old son, Sekou, Chapter 1 also explores the shifting political and economic landscape in Oakland in two periods, from 1960 to 1980 and from 1980 to 2005. Their stories illustrate how Oakland's economy, education, and politics shifted the form and content of activism in these two periods: first, pre-1970s, largely defined by civil rights, black power, and the revolutionary nationalism articulated by the Black Panther Party, and, second, post-1970s, with its activism, largely defined by defense and resurrection of community organizations.

Chapter 2 describes the role of care in the radical healing process. The chapter focuses on two young people's experience of traumatic events in Oakland and how caring relationships encouraged them to engage in community-change activities. The chapter focuses on how Leadership Excellence uses radical healing as a strategy to connect with youth and engage them in community change. From the perspectives of both youth and their adult staff, Chapter 2 explores three critical components of radical healing. First, I illustrate how the organization (1) provides support from traumatic personal events and neighborhood violence, (2) cultivates political identities among black youth by resurrecting a healthy racial and ethnic identity, and (3) provides tools and knowledge for youth to engage in ongoing personal growth need for community change. Based on my 5 years of facilitating weekend workshops, youth retreats, and camps, Chapter 2 is grounded in my firsthand experience of working with black youth in Oakland. I discuss how relationships with adult mentors, political education, and racial awareness transformed black youths' view of themselves as being relatively powerless to change neighborhood conditions as they began to see themselves as powerful community actors in their neighborhood.

Chapter 3 describes how to build the type of community necessary for healing to occur. This chapter traces the experiences of two participants in Leadership Excellence's 5-day personal-transformation camp designed specifically for black youth. Through a detailed account of their activities at Camp Akili and their experiences, the chapter provides portrait of how to navigate and heal from community issues. I highlight the stories of two youth at camp who struggled with racial identity, sexual abuse, and loss caused by violence. I painstakingly take the reader through a series of intense workshops, activities, and discussions during the summer of 2003 that remove the "tough front" from black youth and allow us into a world of intensely personal narratives that reveal their passions, hopes and dreams, how they love, and ultimately their humanity.

Chapter 4 illustrates how fragile and sometimes damaging ideas about black masculinity can be transformed for young black men. This chapter focuses on how to build political consciousness among black young men. It offers a portrait of Marcus and Vince, two 17-year-old men who were required to participate in LE's programs by the Alameda County Office of Probation. Angry, deviant, and sometimes explosive, they were not unlike many young men who walked through the LE's doors. Marcus was known for his gang affiliation and street crimes when he came to LE. Within 6 months, he had developed a refined political identity that he used to confront police brutality on his block. The chapter describes how Marcus and Vince organized a fathers' support group at the local jail so that boys could reconnect to their fathers.

It is rare in qualitative research to be able to describe the impact of a phenomenon over a 10-year period. Many of the youth that I worked with in 1997 are now adults, with full-time jobs, struggling to complete college, with children of their own. Chapter 5 provides a rare look into how three adults describe their lives after participation as youth in LE. Without romanticizing their lives, this chapter illustrates how their trip to Ghana, in

West Africa, shaped their own identity development, political awareness, and sense of activism. One young man became more active in local organizing in Oakland, while another created an activist support group for parenting undergraduate students at the local college she attended. The chapter provides key insights into the ideas, experiences, and skills that really matter for black youth as they enter adulthood.

The concluding chapter poses several provocative and rather unorthodox implications for pedagogy, policy, and practice. I return to the book's thesis and argue that radical healing occurs when black youth build critical consciousness and engage in activities that sustain wellness and facilitate justice. These practices, once identified, can be used to inform social policy, pedagogy in the classroom, and youth development practices.

First, the conclusions focus on specific pedagogical strategies for teachers and youth service providers who work with African American youth. These strategies include ecologically responsive ones that focus on building the capacity of young people to act upon their environment in ways that contribute to well-being for the common good.

Radical healing as a ecologically responsive strategy highlights the socially toxic conditions in urban communities; the process for building the capacity for youth to respond to these conditions; and the ways in which social justice, agency, and resistance can contribute to individual, community, and broader social wellness. One strategy is to understand the local neighborhood by visiting the parks, liquor stores, and bus routes where young people "hang out" when they are not in school. Learning how young people navigate urban space can provide rich and valuable capital in the classroom by making learning more directly relevant to their daily lives. Another strategy is to develop "urban literacy" skills by paying attention to youth culture. For example, the burgeoning Hyphee movement in Oakland is a cultural movement among black youth that integrates dance, style of dress, and language that rejects or resists corporate cooptation and that celebrates freedom of space and style and rejoices in youthfulness. Understanding these cultural shifts provides service providers, teachers, and policy makers key insight into young people's lives outside the school context.

Second, the concluding chapter offers policy recommendations for schools, grassroot organizations, and youth-serving institutions. These recommendations include suggestions such as including youth participation on boards of directors or appropriate governing bodies and training youth to document and research neighborhood issues from their perspective. This provides youth with the skills, knowledge, and opportunity to offer a version of their reality that is often ignored by adult policy makers.

Last, I provide a process for practitioners to develop. Through this, they may implement a pedagogy of healing that includes creating a refuge for black youth, encouraging self-exploration by building racial and ethnic identity, and equipping youth with tools to improve community conditions.

1

A Trip Through a Blues City: Youth, Radicalism, and the Politics of Oakland

OAKLAND IS THE TYPE OF place that some refer to as a "blues city," the gritty, boisterous, working-class cousin to its more glamorous and refined San Francisco.[1] Those of us who live here love the city not for its sophistication, but for its raw unpretentiousness. Living in Oakland reminds us of the truth of urban life: The beauty of the city is not found simply in fancy buildings, glamorous waterfronts, or pristine parks, but rather in people and communities. Despite the city's reputation as crime ridden, dangerous, and violent, Oakland residents can identify with its underdog status and celebrate the phrase that has recently appeared on T-shirts, posters, and even the cover of the new *Oakland Magazine*, "I hella love Oakland." People here love the city for its radical political history, ethnic diversity, commitment to working-class politics, and simply put its "flavor." Just like a good bowl of home-cooked gumbo, once you get a taste of the city, you immediately feel like you're home.

Oakland is divided into two major terrains—the flatlands to the west and the hills in the east of the city (Figure 1.1). The major thoroughfare in the city is East 14th Boulevard, renamed International Boulevard in 1996 to capture the ethnic diversity of the city and to reduce the stigma that had become attached to the city's only major artery. Driving through Oakland on International Boulevard, you see large blocks of industrial space toward the west and residential homes and apartments toward the east. Oakland is a rather narrow city dominated by small, single-family homes that in the 1930s and 1940s were occupied by factory workers. The best way to know Oakland, however, is to ride on the bus, beginning in West Oakland and headed southeast toward East Oakland. On the bus we can point out the city's geographic diversity, cross sections of the city's ethnic neighborhoods,

Figure 1.1. City of Oakland.

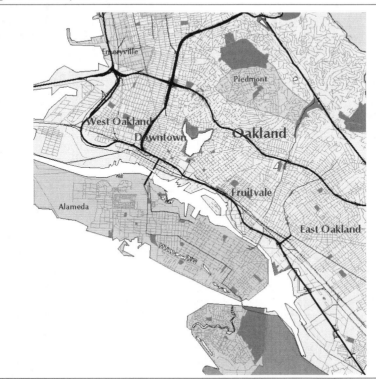

class divisions, new shopping areas and other development projects, and neglected neighborhoods. On our bus ride, I will point out sites (parks, schools, neighborhoods, malls, youth centers) particularly important to the themes raised in this book about African American youth.

West Oakland, our starting point, is the city's oldest neighborhood and is separated from other parts of the city by the downtown district. The streets here are lined with large Victorian homes, many of which have been owned by black families since the 1930s. Known for its rich history as "West Coast Harlem" because of its bustling black-owned businesses, West Oakland once had the largest population in the city. This was largely because of the substantial number of Pullman porters who were hired by the Southern Pacific Company to work as baggage handlers and waiters in dining cars as early as the 1880s. Like many historically black neighborhoods today, the black-owned businesses have been replaced by corner liquor stores; the homes, while grand, are worn and need painting and repairs. On many of the streets there are old storefront churches, liquor stores, and neighborhood markets. Neighborhood residents often shop at these markets and pay twice the amount they would at chain grocery stores. However, there are no major grocery stores in West Oakland; and there are no banks, only check-cashing outlets. Driving down the main thoroughfare, you wouldn't know that the neighborhood has been undergoing dramatic development and gentrification for the past 10 years. Looking out of our bus window, you see mostly black residents carrying out their daily routines, young people hanging out in front of the markets, and elderly residents sitting on their front porches. Most of the development is occurring in the western area of this community, known as the Lower Bottoms. The name accurately describes this area of West Oakland, because of its isolation and concentration of crime and poverty.

In the summer, the streets here are busy all night long with loud car stereos, young folks hanging out on corners, and police breaking up fights. Shootings in the area continue to raise concern among middle-class families about purchasing a home here despite the growing development of condominiums and new homes. As we pass by Defermery Park, groups of local teens hang out, play catch, and joke with each other. Many of the teens throughout the city seem to have a common dress code—baggy jeans and a crisp, clean, white T-shirt accompanied by a black or gray "hoody" (hooded sweatshirt). The park, however, is not the primary gathering place for youth in West Oakland. As in other areas of the city, young people congregate on the corner or along the block where they live.

The block is more than simply a residential geographic boundary. For young people who are restricted from public space in the city, the block serves as a communal gathering place where youth share stories, play, sell goods, and exchange information. The block also provides a geographic identity for some youth. Often young people are known by their name and the name of the neighborhood where they live. I have visited youth in West Oakland without having their exact addresses and simply pulled over to ask youth on the nearby block, "Y'all know where lil Malik stay at? He Cedric's cousin." Without giving an exact address, they would reply, "You mean Malik with the dreads? Yeah, he stay round the corner in the blue house on the left." It is not unusual for youth to identify with their blocks where their families and extended families have resided for decades.

Violence is common here. During the summer months, West Oakland may experience a significant percentage of the shootings in the city. There is a large billboard here that reads, "Who Killed Me?" with the picture of Khadfy, an 18-year-old graduate of nearby McClymonds High School who was shot and killed while riding his bike at the school. Billboards like these are a constant reminder that in Oakland, violent crime is common among black youth. Navigating violence, avoiding "turfs," and staying out of harm's way is increasingly difficult in a city where African American males make up a significant number of all homicides.

Leaving West Oakland, we cross a major freeway that separates West Oakland from downtown. Since 2004, downtown Oakland has witnessed dramatic redevelopment. Prior to 2004, the waterfront, which is part of the downtown corridor, was mostly composed of industrial buildings, manufacturing plants, and storage facilities. Since that time, these industrial buildings have been replaced by lofts, condominiums, and upscale retail outlets catering to young professionals. The downtown core has also experienced the development of more than 10,000 new housing units, mostly condominiums, and 5 modern high-rise buildings to accommodate the rapid growth and expansion of the Bay Area's dot-com economy. Despite the dot-com bust in 2000, three large condominium developments and two high-rise buildings continue to reshape city's skyline. Residents in other areas of the city complained to Mayor Jerry Brown about the uneven development occurring in Oakland. Since 2004, most of the new development had occurred in the downtown corridor without much development in other areas of the city.

In contrast to San Francisco's downtown, where there are bustling crowds of people, downtown Oakland is much slower. People come to downtown Oakland from the suburbs to work, visit city hall to obtain a building permit or clear a traffic ticket, or simply meet for lunch in Jack London Square downtown's waterfront district. Although only blocks from West Oakland, downtown is visibly more diverse in race and class than West Oakland. Here business professionals share the sidewalks with young people, panhandlers, and local merchants. While there are some single-family homes, most have been converted to medical offices that house small dental, chiropractic, or family practices. The downtown streets are lined with mostly small, family-owned businesses, and 1950-style three- or four-story office buildings. On the corner of Broadway and 14th, there is a bus stop where teens wait to transfer to the bus heading north up Broadway to Oakland Technical High School, one of Oakland's six high schools. As they wait for the bus, they are always animated as if they were waiting for a ride at the fair. Two women in business suits try not to make eye contact with these groups of youth as they pass by them on their lunch hour. In fact, many of the business clientele here pay little attention to the groups of youth despite their loud, verbose language. The response that these adults display toward youth in Oakland typifies a fear of black youth in the city, which of course no one wants to admit, not even to themselves.

A friend who works in the downtown area shared with me an incident that happened to her while riding the bus. After finding her seat, she noticed a young black teen harassing an elderly Asian woman who, trying to earn extra money, had several rather large bags of cans she had collected to take to the local recycling center. The young man yelled at the elderly woman, "Move your fucking bags!" The elderly woman moved her bags, and as she did so, he kicked one, spewing crushed cans over the floor of the bus. He laughed and sat down, and no one on the bus looked at him or said a word. My friend who witnessed this was also guilty of being frozen by fear and wanted desperately to say something to the young man about his rude behavior. Instead, like everyone else on the bus, she said nothing.

Despite these tensions, youth and adults frequent the fast food outlets, bookstores, and coffee shops in downtown. Two blocks down Broadway there is a storefront shop—posing as a dentist office—that specializes in gold teeth, gold fangs, and an assortment of "oral jewelry," which has become popular among black youth in Oakland. Youth walk in and out of the store with excitement about their new purchases.

Continuing on, we enter Chinatown, which is located in the downtown area and has a distinctly different appearance. Most of the businesses here display store advertisements in Chinese, and the street signs are in both English and Chinese. Entering Chinatown, we can see a large building that proudly displays the sign "Bank of the Orient." Several new brightly colored buildings house the Asian American Community Center and other small nonprofit organizations all within walking distance of high- and low-rise residential housing. On the corner there is a small child-care center and elementary school. Almost all the children on the playground are Asian. You can always hear the laughter and buzz of children playing near this corner. Not many black youth here, except for a few who are walking through the neighborhood on a shortcut to the nearby community college that marks the outer border of downtown.

Through Chinatown and further down International Boulevard, we enter the San Antonio/Fruitvale districts of Oakland. A large billboard reads, "Sex with a minor is a crime," warning predators that they will be prosecuted for statutory rape. A group of Latino and African American teens, maybe 15 or 16 years old, ride their skateboards in one of the several strip malls that make up the landscape of this section of International Boulevard. This area of the city is composed of small two- to three-bedroom homes and numerous apartment complexes. This is a bustling community lined with taco restaurants, automotive repair shops, Mexican bakeries, clothing stores, and small community organizations. Some of the Mexican men in Fruitvale wear traditional cowboy hats, boots, and jeans, an indication of their southwestern cultural roots. There is a large department store that specializes in Quinceañera dresses for girls. The size of the store and the assortment of brightly colored dresses in the windows are an indication of the community's Mexican culture.

San Antonio/Fruitvale is primarily composed of Latino and Asian working-class families. Since 1990, Oakland has witnessed an exodus of African American families who have relocated to the surrounding suburbs. In 2004, the Fruitvale Transit Village, a three-block retail and residential center that resembles a state-of-the-art Mexican plaza, was constructed to cater to the language and cultural needs of Latino youth. Despite this effort to provide youth in this neighborhood community programs, crime continues to plague the community. In fact, the youth commonly refer to this neighborhood as the "murder dubs"—*dubs* is term that means "20s," meaning the street numbers (21st Street, 22nd Street, 23rd Street) within most of Fruitvale. Some of these dynamics have contributed to tensions between black and Latino communities in the city. Residents say that violence and crime among youth in the area could be more effectively addressed if the city allocated more resources for neighborhood programs. Critics claim that the city's resources are too heavily directed toward African American youth, leaving very little for Latino youth. The tensions between African American and Latino youth are just beneath the surface of race relations among youth in the city. In 1989, rising gun violence and fights between Black and Latino youth in the neighborhood erupted at nearby Fremont High School, which brought citywide attention to the conflicts between Black and Latino youth in the area. While these conflicts have diminished, the tension between youth groups remain.

Continuing south on International Boulevard through San Antonio/Fruitvale, we finally enter East Oakland. While the stores and homes on International Boulevard look the same as in the Fruitvale district, one immediately notices the large number of African Americans. As we cross 66th Avenue, the stores and markets dramatically change from Spanish to English. There are several small storefront churches where during the evening you can hear drums, tambourines, and voices singing gospel music spilling out on streets for those who walk by. On the corner of 81st and International Boulevard, there is a older woman wearing a light blue sweater and carrying grocery bags, waiting for the bus. She can hear the gospel music through the loud traffic, and for a moment she smiles because she recognizes the song coming from the nearby church.

Churches in East Oakland are an important part of the political and cultural landscape of the city because they are perhaps the last bastion of black political infrastructure. There are approximately 150 churches located in East Oakland alone, the largest being Acts Full Gospel, which boasts a membership of 8,000, with more than 2,000 attending on any given Sunday.

Allen Temple Baptist Church, a well-known community staple in East Oakland located on 85th, owns an entire city block, with a community school, senior housing apartments, community center, and several other buildings in East Oakland. About three blocks east from here is Eastmont Mall, Oakland's only shopping mall. In the 1970s, Eastmont Mall was bustling with anchor stores like JCPenney, Mervyn's, Safeway Supermarket, and Woolworth, as well as other small stores that served the vast southeast side of Oakland. Today, however, unlike the case at many malls in America that serve as gathering places for youth, young people don't really hang out here. Eastmont Mall is much more an indoor flea market with few stores. In the 1990s, JCPenney and Mervyn's left, and the reputation of the declining neighborhood convinced many local and suburban residents to stay away. By the mid-1990s, many of the stores were converted into offices for nonprofit community groups, county offices, a health clinic, and a police station.

Continuing on International Boulevard, we pass 98th Avenue, which marks what some youth refer to as "Deep East" Oakland, the last section of Oakland before the neighboring city of San Leandro. Deep East Oakland is mostly composed of small residential homes. One street away, on Bancroft Boulevard, there is Castlemont High School, and next door to the high school is the Youth Uprising youth center. The Youth Uprising center is in a 25,000 square foot state-of-the-art building and offers a wide range of programs and services that develop youth leadership to transform the community.

Deep East Oakland marks the end of the bus ride. While there is only a small sign that signals that you have just left Oakland and entered San Leandro, there is a dramatic change in the residential surroundings that indicate you have entered another city. While you are driving on East 14th and entering San Leandro, the street pavement becomes smoother and devoid of potholes, and the homes that line the street are nestled between nicely manicured lawns and gardens.

There is more to Oakland, however, than its buildings, streets, and houses. There is a rich political and social history that sheds light on how black youth in the city come to make sense of Oakland's streets, schools, and politics. There is a rich and sometimes forgotten history that illustrates how the political ebb and flow in Oakland created opportunities for economic and political mobility only to be closed off mostly to youth. The next section of this chapter will provide a discussion of the youth political culture and the robust political infrastructure in Oakland, which in the late 1960s and throughout the 1970s contributed to vibrant forms of civic and political life for black youth in the city.

BLACK ACTIVISM, 1960 TO 1975

In the period 1965–1975, a broad constellation of political and economic opportunities existed for youth in Oakland, and while far from perfect, these opportunities contributed to a shared sense of political optimism and a feeling that change was possible. This sense of political optimism in Oakland had a profound impact on the political consciousness of black youth and encouraged their involvement with organizations, ideas, and networks of young activists. Availability of jobs, active involvement in civic affairs, and organizational life, as well as a culture of activism, all contributed to a vibrant civic life for black youth in Oakland. This environment also incubated new ideas about justice, birthed the Black Panther Party, and ushered in healing spaces for reflection and care. By 1980, however, fewer jobs, disinvestments in schools, and the growth of the crack economy changed much of this landscape and ultimately transformed the content and form of black youth activism in Oakland. The story of 63-year-old Roland and his 24-year-old son, Sekou, illustrates the shifting terrain in which activism occurred in Oakland.

ROLAND'S ACTIVISM: THE GROWTH OF BLACK YOUTH ACTIVISM IN OAKLAND

I first met Roland at a community meeting on 12th Street in West Oakland in 2002. The meeting was held to organize parents so they could figure out a way to prevent the closure of the West Oakland Community School, where I served on the board of directors. Roland is a well-built, stocky man of few words and dresses with a surprising urban style for a man who is over 60. Equipped with the latest name-brand jeans, hooded sweatshirts, and boots, Roland pulls off the urban aesthetic without the fake veneer that usually signals that someone is "trying" to be cool. Roland is a connoisseur of black popular culture, and after talking to him for 5 minutes, you get the impression that he has been around for a while.

In 1967, Roland was one of the many young community leaders in Oakland who was introduced to politics and activism. His activism was sparked by community concerns about how Oakland would use funds from the new Office of Economic Opportunity (OEO), established by President Lyndon B. Johnson in 1964 to actualize his War on Poverty. Between 1965 and 1970, the federal government established an array of programs and grants directed at eliminating poverty. Oakland pursued the new OEO funding and was successful in receiving twice as much as Los Angeles and more than any other West Coast city (Self, 2003). The influx of federal dollars created badly needed job training and placement centers, adult education, legal assistance, and a host of other educational services for young people in the city (Self, 2003).

Roland and other young community activists wanted to address poverty by creating jobs in Oakland. This strategy was quite different from that of the mostly professional and white members of the Oakland Economic Development Corporation (OEDC), who viewed poverty as a result of lack of motivation. For the OEDC, "poverty was addressed as problem with individual development and the social disorganization of poor communities rather than a function of the distribution of existing jobs or employment segregation" (Self, 2003, p. 201). The philosophical differences about how to address poverty, combined with federal legislation that requiring "maximum feasible participation" of indigenous community members, contributed to a grassroots coup of the OEDC by young black community activists in 1966. With 51% control over the OEDC, the community activists controlled nearly $1.9 million for community-revitalization programs and services and worked quickly to rearticulate the strategies on how to address poverty in the city by focusing on delivering immediate jobs to neighborhoods rather than on an expansion of existing social services (Rhomberg, 2004; Self, 2003). The newly created OEDC focused antipoverty dollars on four "target areas" in Oakland, West Oakland, North Oakland, East Oakland, and Fruitvale. Each of the target areas established antipoverty centers, small neighborhood-based offices where local youth could seek job placement, legal, and other important services. These centers helped to establish a new constituency of young black activists who worked to mobilize the most marginalized and poorest segments of the city. For Roland, the opportunity to control and influence these dollars marked a significant turning point in his life:

> I have lived in Oakland for 40 years and when the OEDC had mostly community folks, we saw it as an opportunity to do something different in the city. We knew that job creation was about opportunities to work and job preparation, not simply motivating people to go find employment.

Perhaps more than any other time in Oakland, the period 1965–1970 witnessed vibrant and robust civic and political life among black youth. As the OEDC grew and focused more on job creation and social services in neighborhoods, Rhomberg noted that these federally subsidized antipoverty centers "became a locus of grassroots political organization in Black and Latino neighborhoods" (2004, p. 143). One of the most significant legacies of the War on Poverty in Oakland was that it unleashed an arsenal of community and grassroots programs and organizations that later contributed to a vibrant civic life for black youth and helped to establish a strong political infrastructure of small grassroots organizations. With a greater focus on hiring neighborhood residents, the OEDC neighborhood programs hired young grassroots community organizers, social work professionals, and civil rights activists who many shared black nationalist views.

Roland was one of these neighborhood activists, who was hired at a local antipoverty center in East Oakland because of his solid community connections and sophisticated knowledge of Oakland community politics. Roland was charismatic, street savvy, and known as someone who could fight. Consequently, he was well respected and had a way of connecting with other young brothas in almost every part of the city. It was primarily, however, through his work at the East Oakland poverty center that he was exposed to political philosophies and organizing skills through older youth in his neighborhood. Roland commented,

> During that time I remember I was selling marijuana to one of these older guys who worked at the center. I remember for some reason I went to their apartment. I didn't even know these guys, but I went to their apartment, and they were playing Gil Scott Heron and started talking about all this political stuff. They would discuss black nationalism and black power and all this which I had never heard about. I was like, what are they talking about? After a few months I began to understand because other folks at the center were talking about similar things. After a while, I started to listen to Gil Scott Heron and it seemed like he was teaching me, and I started to understand more. I remember one dude said, "If I'm gonna die, I want go out fighting for my people." So being around these cats put that fire in me, you know, that resistance.

For Roland, exposure to new political ideas served as a catalyst to learn more about the conditions of black people. Having gone to jail, and witnessing firsthand the ways that the juvenile justice system incarcerated black youth, he was drawn to black nationalist ideas through his connections to activists in the poverty centers. Despite his ongoing involvement in small drug sales and pimping, Roland would promote these ideas even in the context of his illegal activities.

> I used to pimp girls on the street out on MacArthur and Telegraph. I remember talking to one of my girls sitting down. You know, I'm like, "Let's look up the word 'philosophy.'" We would look up the

word "philosophy," and I would say to her, "You could be a philosopher." I'm talking to the girl that I done made into a prostitute about revolutionary nationalism.

In North and West Oakland, the antipoverty centers provided fertile ground and an important infrastructure for the establishment of black power and black nationalist ideas. The writing from Kwame Nkrumah, Franz Fanon, and E. Franklin Frazier helped to further crystallize nationalist strategies among many grassroots organizations in Oakland. Donald Warden, a law student at University of California, Berkeley, and a community activist, established the Afro-American Association in 1962, the first indigenous black nationalist organization on the West Coast (Self, 2003). Through a local radio show, Warden, with assistance from local political activists Paul Cobb and Ron Dellums, "promoted cultural nationalism on college campuses . . . and embraced a nationalism that fused black capitalism, Afro-centrism, and Garveyite self-help" (p. 222)

By 1966, North and West Oakland flourished with a vibrant political and intellectual atmosphere through numerous small political and cultural organizations that focused on black liberation. As Self noted, as early as the 1970s, North and West Oakland were "home to some of the most creative and inspired political projects on the American scene" (2003, p. 223). The Revolutionary Action Movement (RAM), Soul Students Advisory Council, Group to Industrialize the Ghetto (GIG), the McClymonds Youth Council, and in 1966 the emergence of the Black Panther Party for Self Defense not only contributed to a rich vibrant political culture, but also formed a burgeoning political infrastructure for black youth to develop political identities and broader social consciousness about the oppressive conditions in which they lived. In this politically rich environment, Roland and other black youth in Oakland attended political rallies and meetings at Merritt College sponsored by the Afro American Association and regularly engaged in political debates in barbershops and in arguments and conversations about how to achieve black liberation. Despite the fact that there was little consensus and sometimes tensions between these organizations and youth groups, the presence of the groups contributed to perhaps the most robust and vibrant forms of black youth political infrastructure Oakland had ever experienced. Roland commented:

> We had a number of other organizations around during that time. There was GIG, a Group to Industrialize the Ghetto. We had CORE, and a functional NAACP, who could mobilize people. These are groups who could go in the community and thousands of people would show up, because people could relate to what they were

saying. There was also a political structure in the community, a machinelike operation, an apparatus, a political body, a political structure manifest in these particular groups. An organized structure, be it the NAACP, or CORE, or the Black Panther Party. You know, these groups were functional. They were able to tap into these community resources and people and bring people together.

It was in this context that, in 1966, Bobby Seale and Huey Newton formed the Black Panther Party for Self Defense. Frustrated with the inability of the local cultural nationalist organizations to reach the "lumpen proletariat . . . and relate to the brother who's pimping, the brother who's hustling, the unemployed, the downtrodden, the brother who's robbing banks, who's not politically conscious" (Seale, 1970, p. 30), they formed the Black Panther Party. Using the North Oakland Neighborhood Anti-Poverty Center, where Seale and Newton were employed as community organizers, and Bobby Seale's living room, they scoured through books, debating the ideas of Franz Fanon, Che Guevara, Mao Tse-tung and Malcolm X. Concerned with providing jobs and self-defense, Newton and Seale immediately began a strategy to leverage the support and respect they had developed with West and North Oakland youth through work in the antipoverty programs to provide political education and black history to Oakland youth. Seale stated, "Through work in the poverty programs, I was able to meet a lot of the young cats who would later become lumpen proletarians," or the primary political constituents of the Black Panther Party (1970, p. 35).

During the summer of 1967, Roland became more deeply involved with the activities of the party. He recalled:

> I was in Canada with my mom's church when I decided to join the party. My father sent me a *San Francisco Chronicle* newspaper; there was a mail strike in Canada and so the papers were late. Since I was getting the *Chronicle*, all the kids from the Bay Area would come, get around me to see what was happening. So they all came around, and I was opening up the paper. Because of the mail strike, there were about four bundles. I don't know why I picked this particular bundle up, but as I slowly opened it up, the headline said, "Blacks Riot in California." Now I got six white kids standing behind me, and I'm in a Christian environment, right? For the first time in my life, I had an identity crisis. I never will forget this; I went out on the Jarvis street and I prayed, and I said, "God, I'm in the wrong place right now, because what's happening." I came back home to Oakland through Seattle and I went off to Merritt College to join

the Black Panther Party. You know, Huey and David Hilliard would talk to us young brothers all the time, teaching us. We knew we had a purpose and so we pushed on, and that experience was a good experience. It was a very positive experience for me.

The emergence of the Black Panther Party for Self Defense in 1966 reshaped the political and cultural landscape for black youth in Oakland for decades. The Panthers offered a relevant, comprehensive program and ideology that placed poor, working young people's concerns at the center of political analysis. Roland found this ideology and approach to self-determination a dramatic shift in his worldview:

Being in the Black Panthers in the sixties was really about building political consciousness for me. A lot of folks were into Malana Karenga's cultural nationalism; for me it was important to change my mindset. I think we were into a survival mode, as opposed to a recapturing and moving-ahead mode. So we spent a lot of time raising consciousness.

For Roland, the Black Panther Party played an important role not only in fostering political consciousness, but also in developing close relationships with other members who shared a common vision and purpose for their work in Oakland. It was not by accident that Roland was attracted to the Black Panther Party. The black leather jackets worn by party members as well as the ability to talk about everyday issues made joining the party irresistible for young black youth searching for a political identity.

That theme of political identity was core. I later interviewed former Black Panther Party chief of staff David Hilliard, who commented:

Certainly more noticeable is the fact that there is no real voice that speaks to the issue of the underclass, and the most oppressed segment of society. In the sixties and seventies, the Black Panther Party was that vehicle, that gave voice and expression to the Black underclass, which we call the lumpen proletariat. These were the unemployed and the unemployables, the pimps, the prostitutes, and the drug dealers. They were the so-called illegitimate capitalists. We gave expression to that segment of society because that was our targeted group. We organized them, and not since the Black Panther Party has there been any organization that has galvanized that segment of society toward any positive end. So that's really noticeable. You know, those are the kind of things that happened 20, 30 years ago, that are nonexistent.

While there were many organizations that shared black liberation philosophy, these organizations were mostly aimed at black college students and rarely reached out beyond the confines of campus life. The Black Panther Party in Oakland not only considered the black poor and uneducated youth their primary constituency, they conceptualized black youth as the "lumpen proletariat" a term they borrowed from philosophers Karl Marx and Friedrich Engels to convey the idea that the real political power of social movements resides in the masses of people who are the most dispossessed in society. The party also was a catalyst for the burgeoning black youth political consciousness in Oakland. Roland's involvement in political rallies held at parks, the dissemination of newspapers, information about access to jobs through fliers, the creation of important free community services programs, and of course political action, connected him to a vital and vibrant social and political network. This network provided disconnected young people with exposure to important political ideas and concepts; immersion into community organizing; and access to basic needs such as jobs, food, and education. As Hilliard commented:

> We were building a community infrastructure and we wanted control of the institutions in our communities. Huey Newton would say that a community is a comprehensive collection of institutions. An institution of course is a bank or church or school. For the most part, however, African Americans do not control these institutions. I'm not defining a community just by virtue of its physical space, but also in terms of educational, economic, and cultural control of ideas and resources. In the earlier years, we were really trying to manifest our 10-point program, and were able to realize some of the social service programs, i.e., free health clinics, medical programs. We were able to replicate that in some 40 cities in America, where we actually did sickle cell anemia testing, and hypertension testing, and brought these free health-care services in the community for people who could not afford medical health care.

Being connected to the Black Panther Party also meant being connected to a network of black men who could support one another with finding work. Between 1968 and 1978 many of the jobs available to black young men were in manufacturing. Jobs ranging from those in trained technical trades such as the ones held by merchant seamen who worked in Oakland's shipyard or naval base, to less skilled jobs in the factories, were plentiful and available to young black men in Oakland. Hilliard reflected on his experience with finding employment in Oakland as a young man:

There were jobs around back then. Mostly labor-type jobs like the Chevrolet plant which was here in Northern California. Most of my friends worked at the Chevrolet plant, or General Motors, you know, making a pretty decent living, and were able buy homes, and have a pretty decent living. Jobs were more plentiful, you know, coming up as a young man, I could work. There was a Coca-Cola factory in Oakland, over on 14th Street. There was also Nabisco Shredded Wheat, Granny Goose potato chips, Gerber baby foods, Hunt's, and the Del Monte cannery. All these were in Oakland. Anybody that wanted a job during the summer months, from about May through August, could go work at the various factories and canneries. Del Monte's, Hunt's. Many people worked during fruit season, and would draw unemployment until the canneries opened up again.

The presence of work in Oakland provided youth with viable options to earn money. Despite the fact that some of these jobs were low paying and required few skills, they were important in that work was integrated into daily life (Hilliard & Cole, 1993). It was common for young men in Oakland to work at a local factory. In our interview, Hilliard discussed the availability of jobs:

As a young guy in Oakland, I worked various manual jobs. It was a lot easier in the sixties, because Oakland had an industrial base. Oakland had the military base, the navy base, the army base, and a lot of Oakland residents worked in some way for the industrial-military complex in the city. I didn't work for the navy base or the army base, I worked as a young guy with the Longshoremen's Association. You know, one of the more permanent jobs was [with] the International Longshoremen and Warehousemen Union. It was a period where there were good-paying union jobs in the city. If they really wanted to become an apprentice, they could go to the construction unions and, you know, go into some of these training programs and be an apprentice carpenter. Of course the labor unions were also very—very discriminatory.

The availability of jobs in Oakland during this period signifies a time of economic ebb and flow. The constellation of government jobs such as at the Alameda Naval Air Station, the Oakland Army Base, and Oak Knoll Naval Hospital were all important sources of employment for blacks in Oakland. Roland and other black youth during this period enjoyed both part- and full-time work and viewed these jobs as temporary employment

options. Roland learned who was hiring and whom to use as a good refer-
ence through connections and relationships within the Black Panther Party.
These relationships, combined with a variety of grassroots political organizations, political ideas, and a culture of activism formed an important
infrastructure (organized set of ideas, organizations, and resources) for
black youth in Oakland that rendered political change possible. Also important to black political culture was the presence of black-owned businesses. They were significant not only to blacks in the city because of their
economic health, but also because they fostered entrepreneurialism within
the black community. Roland commented:

> When I was in high school, some grocery stores were Asian owned,
> but the liquor stores or the restaurants, the nightclubs, the diners
> were owned by blacks. We did have somewhat of an economic base
> in those areas, though I'm not sure why. Now you're hard pressed
> to find a black store owner, a black restaurant owner, for that
> matter in Oakland. That was not the case when I grew up. We had
> movie theaters on 7th Street, there were, I think there were two
> movie theaters on 7th Street, a bowling alley on 7th Street where the
> post office is now located. Everything on 7th Street was black-
> owned! A black theater down there on San Pablo, called the Rialto.
> We had nightclubs, like the Continental nightclub, we had Sweet's
> Ballroom, we had the Shalimar on Sacramento in Berkeley. So you
> had these places that were black owned, and it had this sense of
> black culture and sense of black economic development. We also
> had black dentists and black physicians in the community. So you
> had a sense of community and some sense of economic develop-
> ment. That is nonexistent. Those are some very real, concrete
> changes or developments, you know, over the last 20 years.

Roland's reflections on youth activism in Oakland prior to 1980 highlight at least three key ideas. First, participation in neighborhood politics
through OEDC employment centers exposed him to new political ideas,
and connections to other political organizations. The development of his
political consciousness ultimately led him to the Black Panther Party where
he became deeply involved with local activism. Second, the availability
of jobs in Oakland contributed to a working-class culture in which work,
either full time or part time, was a normal component of everyday life
for black young adults. The connections to jobs were often facilitated
through relationships in black political organizations. Third, a culture of
activism in popular music, public events on campus, and political activities all helped to shape his political consciousness.

Oakland's black political infrastructure provides an important back-drop for understanding youth activism in Oakland. Through its numerous community programs—free breakfast, a community school, free clothing, community clinics, and grocery giveaways—the Black Panther Party confronted the material reality of poverty in Oakland, but what was equally important was the deeper more spiritual, communal, and ideological meaning that the party represented. Its presence signified far more than resistance to violence; for Oakland's youth it fostered a new vision of the ghetto, "alive with possibilities, confident and assertive for a newfound capacity to shape the world" (Self, 2003, p. 233). The party forced youth in Oakland to dream about a world that they could create and imagine a communal way of life and new visions of political possibilities.

THE URBAN TRIFECTA: DISMANTLING OAKLAND'S BLACK POLITICAL INFRASTRUCTURE

By 1970, unfortunately, these forms of vibrant political activity would come under intense attack. In 1970–1980 the robust political infrastructure available to black youth in Oakland began to erode, leaving few opportunities for black youth to develop and engage in meaningful political and civic life. Perhaps the three most significant threats to Oakland's rich political environment were the demise of the Black Panther Party, the exodus of blue-collar jobs, and the influx and spread of crack cocaine. Combined, these factors created a perfect storm, which I call the "urban trifecta" and which transformed the nature of black radialism in urban America.

In 1970, the Federal Bureau of Investigation, in cooperation with the Central Intelligence Agency, formed a special counterintelligence program (COINTELPRO) that worked closely with Oakland police to disrupt the activities of the Black Panther Party. The activities of the party prompted FBI director J. Edgar Hoover to label it the greatest threat to the internal security of the country. By 1972, a significant number of the party's members either were imprisoned or had been killed. By the end of the decade, the majority of FBI counterintelligence operations directed against black liberation groups were aimed at the Black Panther Party. In 1969, the CIA and FBI had raided numerous party offices and had arrested more than 300 leaders of the party. By 1972, the party had become infiltrated by FBI operatives, which contributed to internal fighting, mistrust among members, and in some cases outright illegal activities. In 1974 under the leadership of Elaine Brown, the party faced enormous legal battles and ultimately could not survive the decline in national membership (Hilliard & Weise, 2002; Seale, 1970).

Dramatic economic shifts and the resulting loss of jobs also eroded the black political infrastructure in Oakland. If its black political infrastructure was in part sustained by the presence of jobs for young people, the exodus of these jobs helped to destroy it. In 1980, major employers such as Ford, General Motors, Borden Chemical, and others began efforts to relocate in the surrounding suburbs (Lemke-Sentinel, 1997). Seeking cheaper land, more space, and fewer union problems, large employers relocated from Oakland to nearby areas such as San Leandro, Hayward, and Union City, making it more difficult for young blacks to secure stable work. By 1985 Oakland had lost 24,000 jobs, resulting in mass unemployment for blacks, which further weakened the radical political infrastructure. The jobs that did remain often were low-wage, unstable jobs that did not offer benefits necessary to raise a family. While the exodus of jobs created high unemployment among blacks in the city, a second trend that emerged was the preponderance of low-wage employment (Pitts, 2006). As Pitts noted, in 1970 only 11.7% of full-time employed black men in Oakland earned low wages. By 2000, that number had dramatically increased, to 21%.

With fewer job opportunities, and a growing concern for immediate solutions to make ends meet, many young blacks became increasingly skeptical about the ability of the Black Panther Party and other organizations to deliver jobs that could pay enough to raise a family. The impact of long-term unemployment, leaving few options for viable work, was devastating for black families. By 1985, the exodus of livable-wage jobs, coupled with the preponderance of low-wage service jobs in industries such as fast food and retail prompted many youth to turn to a new economy in Oakland that would guarantee steady income, with opportunities to earn more than any job could offer. Perhaps the final blow to Oakland's black radical infrastructure was the widespread sale of crack cocaine. As early as 1970, a drug culture in Oakland had been well established and was limited to pockets of East and West Oakland. On the streets, heroin was the most common drug, sought by a relatively dedicated, yet small, number of drug users. Controlled by Felix Mitchell, a legendary drug lord whose life and death continue to fascinate Oakland residence, heroine sales dominated Oakland's drug economy. It wasn't until Mitchell's death in 1986 that Oakland's drug economy would begin to dramatically alter community, family, and civic life, exerting its influence for decades.

Without Mitchell's leadership and organizational structure, which provided remarkable control over Oakland's drug economy, young teens without other viable options to earn money turned to "freelance" drug sales without clear leadership and decentralized distribution. Without Mitchell's 69th Street mob, young drug entrepreneurs began vying for drug turf, which resulted in unprecedented violence, causing murders mostly among black youth. The emergence of crack cocaine in the early 1980s intensified these battles. In 1988, drug dealers recognized the demand for a simple form of smokable cocaine. Unlike freebase cocaine, which was difficult and expensive to produce, crack was easy to manufacture in kitchens and substantial amounts could be produced from just one or two grams of cocaine powder. "Early crack markets provided the opportunity for ownership, control and autonomy to anyone who could afford to purchase even a minimal amount of cocaine" (Brownstein, 1996, p. 38).

In Oakland, the crack epidemic delivered a major blow to black civic life among youth and their families. J. Alfred Smith, a longtime resident of Oakland and pastor of Allen Temple Baptist Church commented:

> Crack was an equal opportunity destroyer. Businessmen who dabbled on weekends, thinking they could handle crack, became handled by crack. They joined the barely visible multitude stretching soiled hands to total strangers and begging for spare change. . . . East Oakland was an asphalt jungle sealed by razor-wire fences. Black men of every hue stood in the shadows of the liquor stores nursing cans of cold beer and the pungent aroma of marijuana floated on the morning breeze. This was more than poverty. This was the violent death of the human spirit. (2004, p. 138)

The crack wave that hit Oakland, as in other major cities, fractured families; ruptured the vibrant fabric of black community life; and slowly smothered the visions of justice, hope, and opportunity that had once placed Oakland youth at the center of the black liberation movement. Unfortunately, the widespread use of drugs in Oakland ultimately led to Huey Newton's death in West Oakland in 1989.

PEACE OUT TO REVOLUTION!
POST-1980S ACTIVISM IN OAKLAND

By the early 1980s, Oakland's political scene had dramatically changed for black youth. The destruction of the Black Panther Party, few opportunities for viable employment, and the availability of crack cocaine all contributed to the decline of black radicalism in the city. The Oakland that Sekou experienced was dramatically different from the Oakland that his father Roland knew. By the 1990s, Oakland, like many cities, faced a number of critical issues that threatened to unravel public well-being and safety. First, Oakland faced one of the worse budget shortfalls in a decade. California had cut major dollars from state spending, creating drastic shortages in local municipalities. The state cuts meant a $34 million deficit for

Oakland and, as a result, the city manager, along with Mayor Elihu Harris, called for a salary freeze for all city employees. Second, homicides among young African Americans were rising. By 1992, Oakland had 175 homicides, the highest number in the city's history. Third, there was the exodus of major employers who had provided a financial base for the city's tax revenues.

These issues formed the content and structure of activism for Sekou. His years of private school and his exposure to black nationalist ideas through his family immediately gives one the impression that Sekou has been groomed for activism. It might be easy to confuse him with a 16-year-old high school student because he usually wears a backpack and his short stature and boyish face makes him look much younger than 21. Sekou comes from a large activist family in Oakland; almost everyone in the city knows somebody from the Fielding clan.[2] In the 1970s, the Fieldings were prominent members of the Black Panther Party and were instrumental in the Third World Liberation Front's strike at San Francisco State University, which led to the nation's first black studies department. Sekou commented:

> My mom got me interested in the Black Panthers at an early age because Huey Newton and my mom's brothers used to hang out and get drunk. They used to come through our grandma's house and my grandma would cook for everybody. My folks knew Huey Newton but not for political stuff but just on the social level. The Panthers used to just come around on the block, and eat and talk to my grandma. She didn't know what the Black Panthers really stood for. My mom was more involved with the political stuff, that's how I got aware of politics and stuff going on with black people in Oakland.

There were few distinctions between political life and social life in Oakland's black community in the 1960s liberation movements. After 1986, however, Sekou, like many young people in Oakland, had to navigate in his activist circles without losing his street credibility. On the one hand Sekou was raised with a deep understanding of his family's rich political history, while on the other, he was pulled into the lure of the drug economy and turf wars.

> When I was about 10 years old my brother got caught up in the turf thing and was sentenced to a lot of time in jail. I wanted to help him by getting in the streets to represent him as his little brother. When I went to visit him in jail, I saw that almost everyone in jail, and the

court system, was black! It was just like slavery or something! When he got out of jail all my brother could do was sell weed because he didn't have any other skills. I felt like they still had him enslaved because all he knew was selling weed and the streets.

Roland knew that if Sekou attended the neighborhood high school, he would most likely follow the same path as his older brother. The streets and schools in Oakland by 1992 had got progressively more dangerous for African American boys. Of the 175 homicides in Oakland in 1992, 61%, or 106 victims, were black men (Figure 1.2). More than 50% of the homicide victims were between the ages of 18 and 30. Of the known suspects, 68% were young black men (Burt, 1993). The 175 homicides in Oakland in 1992 stand in stark contrast to just 66 in 1970 (Figure 1.3), when Roland was completing high school.

It was difficult for Roland to completely understand lethal violence among youth in Oakland. In his day, fights were common, but using lethal weapons was rare. Leaving Sekou in a public school in Oakland could get him caught up with the wrong crowd and pulled into the streets; the thought of Sekou becoming a name and homicide number in the newspaper frightened Roland. So his decision to send Sekou to a private school was easy for him. However, he also knew that he had raised his son to resist

Figure 1.2. Oakland homicide suspects and victims by race, 1992.

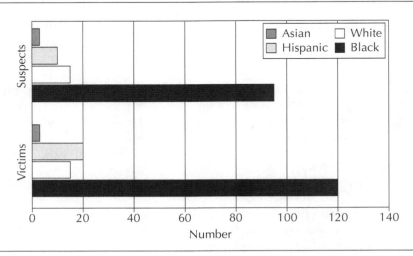

Source: Burt, 1993.

Figure 1.3. All Oakland homicide victims, 1970–1992.

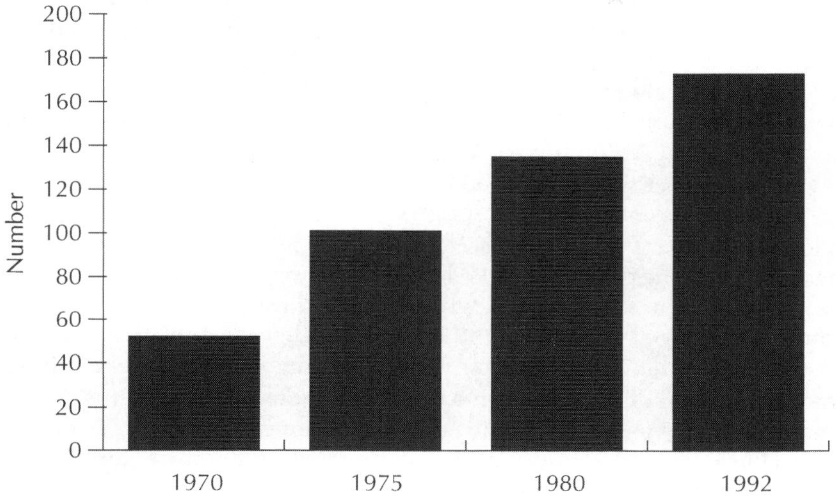

Source: Oakland Police Department, 2008.

injustice and racism, which could be difficult in a private school environment. Sekou resisted the idea of going to private school:

> I felt like it was a contradiction for him to send me to a private school with mostly whites after all this black revolutionary stuff we would talk about. So I felt like, Why can't I go to a black school? I had buddies from the neighborhood that went to public school. Once I started going, I intentionally acted up. I would pick fights, get into arguments, I was one of rowdiest kids at the school. For the most part, I wanted to get kicked out of the school because I never wanted to go to that school.

Despite Roland's best efforts to shield his son from Oakland's violence, Sekou seemed to be drawn to neighborhood friends who were earning a good deal of money from small drug sales on the corner where they would congregate daily. Despite his father's warning to stop hanging out on the corner, Sekou continued to spend time with his longtime neighborhood friends after school there. During this time, Sekou experienced a series of life-threatening events.

I know this young guy named Gary who was told by these older guys to go to a party in West Oakland and shoot it up. He went and shot at the party, and hundreds of people ran, left clothes, shoes, everything, people ran and were getting trampled over, and he injured a lot of people. The older dudes that had him go out and do this got concerned that Gary would snitch and rat them out. So they set Gary up. They told him to meet them at a certain place and they did a drive-by on him. That's why we have that big billboard of all black males who been killed, no females, just black males, at least 25 to 30 males on this billboard.

It wasn't until his life was threatened by people from a rival neighborhood that he reconsidered where to spend time after school. After the incident with Gary, Sekou found himself in other scary situations. He was walking with his cousin not far from his home when he saw a van with men in ski masks slowly approaching them. Sekou recalled his reaction:

I hesitated and we stopped, just completely stopped walking. I thought that they were all gonna jump out on us. If we run, they're going to shoot us, and if we stand here they'll beat us! So we just stood there and hoped that they would fully acknowledge that we ain't one of fools they're looking for. I was in fear because I thought it was over!

After that experience, Sekou stayed in his house except for going to school and making occasional visits. He entertained himself with his PlayStation and decided that hanging out outside on the block wasn't worth his life. After school he came home, and he rarely went to parties in the neighborhood for fear of violence:

After that, I felt unsafe a lot. I basically would try to stay in the house and play PlayStation 2. I have a 61-inch big screen so we can watch movies and play games. I didn't go outside and hang out because it's easy to get caught up in trouble and get shot in broad daylight. So mostly, I didn't do too much after school. I stopped going out to parties.

The presence of violence in Oakland after 1990 fostered a culture of isolation among youth, families, and communities. In attempts to avoid violence, parents shifted their children to safer schools, young people rarely congregated in malls or attended parties and social functions, and neighborhoods rarely came together to build the social ties that bind and build communities. Sekou's choice to spend most of his time indoors playing video games was not a unique phenomenon. In fact, many parents say that they would rather have their children inside where it is safe rather than running the streets where it is unsafe.

Intensified isolation was one of the major forces that influenced post-1980s activism in Oakland. By 1995, youth had become disconnected from parks and venues such as Lake Merritt; rarely visited friends from different parts of the city for fear of territorial retaliation; and avoided Eastmont Mall, the city's only shopping mall. The threat of violence slowly eroded the networks among youth, communities, and institutions. In response to widespread violence, the Oakland police responded with tactics that exacerbated already tense relationships between black youth and police officers. These tactics resulted in greater repression, restriction, and containment of young people in the city.

Between 1995 and 2000, Oakland hired additional police officers to confront violence. Mayor Elihu Harris and the police chief launched a new assault on crime, which further restricted the movement of young people and intensified misconduct. Misconduct among the police was widespread, but most serious among a particular group of 12 officers. For years, black youth have voiced concern about the mistreatment they received from the police (MacDonald, 2004). These allegations of misconduct on the part of the Oakland Police Department are not unfounded. In fact, in 2002 several members of the department were formally charged with willful misconduct and were removed from their posts (Lee, 2004). The tensions contribute to a wide mistrust of police and the justice system on the part of black youth. Sekou recalls an interaction with the police that had become familiar among many black youth in Oakland:

> We were coming from a basketball game at Saint Joe's High School. After the game, we were driving on East 14th, and the police stopped us and told us that they thought we were buying coke (cocaine) or something. So the task force car rushed in to check us out. The problem was, we didn't have anything on us, and there was nothing in the car. They illegally searched the car and did not find anything because we weren't doing anything wrong. We told the officers that we knew our rights, and we knew that they did not have the right to check our car. The officer must have not expected us to talk about our rights so he handcuffed us and slammed us on the hot hood of the police car that they had been driving around all day. It was so hot, it was burning our face!

Stories of police harassment are common among black youth in Oakland. Some officers in the police department acknowledge that they view black youth in the city as a threat to civic order. Oakland's policing tactics focused almost entirely on targeting young African American males and establishing a presence on the streets by public displays of repression. For the department, greater force and more personnel were needed to confront violence in the city. Between 2000 and 2005, Oakland's citizen review board filed 483 complaints of excessive use of force and verbal misconduct by police (Office of the City Administrator, 2005).

Much of what we understand about the decline in activism in the post–civil rights era points to government repression of black radical groups. However, the scope of repression is often limited to the period from 1966 to 1970. While federal efforts to disrupt the activities of organizations like the Black Panther Party may have been explicit in 1966, local policing practices in Oakland by 1980 continued the legacy of repression of black youth. Hostilities between black youth and police in Oakland have fostered distrust in the police department itself; however, more broadly, black youth do not entirely trust the political system (local, state, and federal government) that has supported these policing practices. This trend is not unique to Oakland. Studies have documented the ways in which black youth develop negative attitudes toward and views of the police (Fine et al., 2003).

Because of the numerous experiences of being questioned and stopped by police officers in the city, Sekou and his friends openly discuss their lack of trust in police officers in Oakland. Sekou's close friend Johnathan commented:

> I'm just utterly disgusted when I see police. I don't have positive thoughts when I see them. I was driving the other day and a police car pulled up next to me and I always got this sinking feeling. It was probably because I didn't have my driver's license, so he had a legitimate reason to take me to jail. But even now, even now with my license, I still just don't feel good when they are around me, but just seeing them makes me really sick.

Black youth are suspicious of institutionalized, electoral politics and resentful of state-sponsored institutions because of negative experiences with police and hostility in schools. This is largely because the police, and perhaps schools, have the most contact with black youth. Over time, black youth in Oakland lose faith in state-sponsored institutions that do not work on their behalf. Despite the fact that many young people can point to cousins, aunts, and uncles who had participated in the struggle for black liberation in Oakland, the loss of jobs, impact of crack cocaine, and continued police repression all have contributed to a belief in institutional politics as usual.

MORE SERVICES, LESS ACTIVISM

By 1985, Oakland's growing nonprofit sector had funneled black activists into social support programs and organizations, which further weakened Oakland's black radical infrastructure. The post-1980s witnessed a plethora of social service agencies, city-supported social services and county health programs directed at supporting the children and families who had been most affected by nearly 15 years of joblessness, crime, and substance abuse. Mentoring programs, employment and job training programs, and after-school academic programs replaced many of the activist organizations that had contributed to activism in the city. Many of these programs struggled to find traction among Oakland youth, who navigate daily the landmines left behind by crack cocaine, job loss, and violence. From 1985 to 1995, federal social service expenditures nearly doubled in California (California Department of Finance, 2005). These funds were used primarily to support health and human services. This growth, however, can be seen in the expansion of the number of nonprofit organizations in the San Francisco Bay Area. During the same period, there was an approximately 31% increase in the number of nonprofit organizations in California (California Department of Finance, 2005; Independent Sector, 2001; National Center for Charitable Statistics, 2006).

The expansion of the nonprofit sector was the result of programs that appeared to meet the moral demands of the 1960s movements but siphoned the latter's radical elements into social support "without actually yielding much by way of tangible gains" (Piven & Cloward, 1979, p. 31). In fact, many of today's teachers, community outreach advocates, department directors, supervisors, and program managers were active participants in the Bay Area's black liberation movements. Despite the fact that Oakland has numerous churches, community-based organizations, and civic organizations that provide after-school tutoring, mentoring, and recreation, many of these programs and services continue to struggle with the depth and breadth of issues young people bring to them. While such programs and services are important in the daily survival of youth and their families, those of us who work closely with Oakland's youth understand that these services were necessary, but grossly insufficient. Programs such as tutoring, mentoring, and sports struggled to keep black young people engaged and connected to their services.

Combined, these issues have also threatened perhaps the most important aspect of black civic life for youth, which is, of course, the capacity to dream and imagine a new way of living. More significant than the destruction of Oakland's black radical infrastructure has been the ways in which the crack epidemic has fostered an attack on hope, which in itself can revive a radical civic life. As Robin Kelly eloquently points out, "The 'movement' was more than sit-ins at lunch counters, voter registration campaigns, and freedom rides; it was about self-transformation, changing the way we think, live, love and handle pain" (2002, p. 11). For youth in Oakland, the erosion of the black radical infrastructure rendered hope, vision, and self-transformation intangible and out of reach.

2

Fostering Caring Relationships for Social Justice

There is no political cure for an existential problem.
— Cornel West, *Restoring Hope*

I HAVE ALWAYS LOVED autumn in Oakland. Waking up to see yellow beams of sunshine peering through my bedroom window is always a hint that the day will be blessed with warm breezes that stretch out into a golden lazy afternoon. Walking outside my home in East Oakland, I can hear the birds chirping, and sometimes I can smell freshly cut grass from my neighbor's home, which reminds me of how little time I seem to have to tend to my own overgrown yard.

It was nearly 70 degrees, and it was only 10:00 a.m., and as on most days, my calendar was full. I had several meetings to attend and a visit to a young person's home, and I had to prepare for a youth discussion group for Saturday morning. So I excused myself for taking more time than usual to get to the Leadership Excellence youth center in downtown Oakland.

When I arrived at work, my day began rather uneventfully. I read my e-mails, combed through the mail, and checked my voice mail. I found it strange that Mikayla, one of the youth, had left an urgent message for me to give her a call over the weekend. But before I could complete listening to the other messages, my cell phone rang. Mikayla's worried and tired voice was on the other end. She explained to me that over the weekend, she and her partner, Rena, had been involved in a shooting and she was scared because she had witnessed everything that happened. When she arrived at the youth center about 30 minutes later, she was visibly upset. Immediately, Lisa, a long-term Leadership Excellence employee, stopped working to talk to her and find out what had happened.

It turns out that late Saturday night she and a friend had been driving around with a few guys they knew from school. Even though they really didn't know the guy driving the car, they had seen him around the neighborhood. She explained that they had just left a party in North Oakland when they decided to get a late night bite from Kwik Way's Burgers. When they pulled into the parking lot at Kwik Way's Burgers, they noticed that their driver was staring at someone in a car parked in the lot. Not thinking much of it, Mikayla and Rena exited the car to use the bathroom and purchase their food. Upon returning to the back seat of the car, they saw their driver hop out and swiftly walk to the driver's side of the other car in the parking lot. They watched as he pulled a gun from his jacket, pointed the gun, and shot the driver in the head at near point-blank range. He ran back to the car, where Mikayla and Rena were sitting in the backseat in shock, and quickly sped away before anyone could see what had happened. As Mikayla and Rena were yelling at him, he pulled the car over, looked at them in the backseat, and said, "I know where you live, so you better not say nothing to anyone . . . now get out!" That's when Mikayla called me, because she didn't know exactly what to do. Going to the police could get her killed and put her family in jeopardy. However, not being able to tell anyone made her physically sick. So she simply reached out for help in a dark situation.

We embraced Mikayla, with compassion and love, and created a space for her to share her fears and concerns without judgment and telling her what she needed to do. We knew that if she went to the police she could be in danger. Despite the fact that she witnessed what happened and knew who was involved, being labeled a snitch was a death sentence in Oakland. Recently there had been several shootings involving youth witnesses to crimes. Perhaps the most significant thing we could do for her at the time was to provide a safe place to listen.

This chapter highlights how care can foster activism for young people who experience trauma in their communities. Through in-depth interviews of three youth and participant observations of young people who participated in an after-school program for 2 years with Leadership Excellence, I illustrate, through the grounded experiences of young people, the ways that urban issues such as violence and institutional failure prevent young people from healing from traumatic events. Often trauma and the inability to heal from it are significant barriers to academic success, civic participation, and general health and well-being. The trauma caused by unimaginable choices, however, can be healed. This chapter examines how caring relationships, political consciousness, and action all contribute to healing and well-being for youth who experience trauma in their communities.

Trauma, in this sense, is not simply a single act of violence, but more often ongoing exposure to life threatening experiences. The term *posttraumatic stress disorder* (PTSD) is commonly used to diagnose and describe individuals who have witnessed violence, such as riots, gang shootings, torture, or bombings. However, the term fails to capture the nuance and complexity of the ongoing trauma that urban youth experience. This is largely because the prefix *post* suggests that the traumatic events are in the past and because the focus is almost entirely on events rather than environments. A broader understanding of trauma captures not only the event, but also the community's response and how violence is treated in the general public (Washington, 2007).

For example, one of the most significant difficulties black youth experience is the way in which trauma in black communities is treated by the general public. Embedded in newspapers and in evening news accounts of violence in urban black communities is the notion that violence in black communities is entirely the fault of the people in the neighborhood. Johnson (1995) argues that crime statistics and research tends to reflect and reaffirm racist notions that black communities, and therefore black people, are more violent than whites. Victims of violence events are framed by the media in such a way as to suggest that they deserve their fate. Rather than discussing how years of disinvestment in black communities has created joblessness, for example, the general public asks, "Where is the tragedy?"

> The tragedy of homicides among Blacks is negated in this suggested framework of crime and violence. Violence becomes the word that both subsumes one event (the tragedy of the victim's death) and qualifies another action (a brutal homicide). In addition, this framework defines the actors as potential menaces to society, thereby undermining any sympathy when lives are taken by an act of violence. As a result, the public feels a macabre sense of relief when it is reported that the "menaces" kill each other. Death framed as violence begs the question, "Where is the tragedy?" This framework leaves no room to mourn a family member lost to a brutal death. On an even more insidious level, the "violent" framing of African American homicide incriminates both the assassin and the deceased. Looking at death only through a lens of violence generates silence around the issue of this death as loss. Thus, the tragedy and overall impact of death felt by surviving African American adolescents is hidden by mainstream society's inability and unwillingness to deal with the issue of death or with the brutal way most Black adolescents encounter death. . . . In this harsh light and harsher silence stands the African American adolescent whose friend or loved one was gunned down. (p. 219)

Without a more critical understanding of the root causes of truama, black youth internalize these feelings and blame only themselves or their communities for their conditions. These feelings often are barriers to action. Caring relationships, however, can confront hopelessness and foster beliefs about justice among young people. These caring relationships are not simply about trust, dependence, and mutual expectations. Rather, they are political acts that encourage youth to heal from trauma by confronting injustice and oppression in their lives. Care builds hope, political consciousness, and the willingness to act on behalf of the common good. Care in this sense says, "Because I care about black people, I care about you," and it views each person as vital to a collective struggle for liberation. But young people must heal before they can act.

CARE AS A POLITICAL ACT IN BLACK COMMUNITY LIFE

Often in black communities, beliefs about care, healing, and justice are found in the confines of the church. Sometimes, however, ideas about care, healing, and justice can be found in some aspects of civic life. Sullivan noted, "In cities ravaged by alcohol, cocaine, heroin addictions, and the nexus of the HIV/AIDS pandemic, networks of care, support, and counseling are some of the strongest, most vibrant, and most visible civic infrastructures existing in poor communities and neighborhoods" (1997, p. 1). The destruction of a healthy political infrastructure in black communities across America has in many ways threatened modes of care and justice that historically have played an important role in black social networks and activism. Increasingly, neighborhood-based organizations in black communities have come to recognize the role of care, healing, and justice in developing young people as well as fostering strong, vibrant community life.

Care has become particularly important, given that the state, which once provided basic social services, has failed to address these issues in black communities (Wacquant, 1998). In response to the state's neglect of facilitating basic social welfare, some community organizations have come to serve as a buffer to mitigate what Wacquant (2001) refers to as the "penal state"—the omnipresent influence of state institutions such as police, schools, and prisons that in concert encroach upon urban life through surveillance, zero-tolerance policies, and imprisonment in the name of public safety. Rather than building mutual trust, democratic participation, and community building, Wacquant argues, the penal state threatens the vitality of networks of care in black communities. Scholars have argued that growing poverty, crime, and violence, as well as the state's diminishing role in providing basic social services, has resulted in new forms of social capital in urban black neighborhoods (Dance, 2002). These new forms of social capital are much less concerned about how social networks are fostered and sustained through membership to civic and social organizations and much more focused on how "humane investments" of care contribute in healing and justice among African American youth (p. 84). Caring is one important aspect of social relationships between youth and adults. These caring relationships make possible the achievement of certain ends that would not be attainable (Dance, 2002).

Care among black youth, however, is more than simply trusting relationships and mutual expectations and bonds between individuals. Rather, care within black communities and among youth is viewed as a collective and individual responsibility. The emphasis of care in black communities is on cultural, communal, and political solidarity in addition to interpersonal relationships (Thompson, 1995). Thompson notes that care means "promoting cultural integrity, communal and individual survival, spiritual growth, and political change under oppressive conditions" (p. 29). In communities ravaged by violence, crime, and poverty, care is perhaps one of the most revolutionary antidotes to urban trauma, because it ultimately facilitates healing and a passion of justice. Without investments in caring relationships, young people internalize trauma, which can hinder their capacity to transform the very conditions that created it. Care within the black community is as much a political act as it is a personal gesture: It requires that relationships prepare black youth to confront racism and view their personal trauma as a result of systemic social problems.

For example, the capacity for African American youth to develop a political understanding of racism can promote wellness and healthy development (Ward, 2000; Watts, Williams & Jagers, 2002). Janie Ward (2000) notes that "addressing racism in an open and forthright manner is essential to building psychological health among African American youth" (p. 58), who have been failed by schools, social supports, and traditional youth development programming. In the context of economic decay, political isolation, and urban violence, care is cultivated through ties with adult community members and facilitated by building collective interests through political racial consciousness among black youth. Care in this context moves beyond coping and surviving and encourages black youth to thrive and flourish as they transform community conditions.

This way of conceptualizing care also builds from prior treatments of social capital that focus on the ways in which mutual trust facilitates community action (Ginwright & Cammarota, 2007). Building from Sampson and Raudenbush's (1999) discussion of collective efficacy, which highlights how linkages of trust and willingness act on behalf of the common good, ideas about care and social capital conjoined point to the ways in which trust and political consciousness translate into community action.

LEADERSHIP EXCELLENCE: BUILDING ACTIVISM THROUGH CARE

From Telegraph Avenue in downtown Oakland, it would be easy to miss the Leadership Excellence office, flanked by a beauty shop to the left and a Chinese takeout to the right. There are no large signs, posters, or billboards that announce the organization's precise location, only a glass door marked "1736 Telegraph" and a small black marquee next to a call box that lists three tenants in the building—AMN Architecture, first floor; Tagagi Engineering, second floor; Leadership Excellence, third floor. Entering the small foyer of the building, visitors can sometimes smell the chemicals coming from the beauty shop or the fried vegetables from the Chinese takeout next door, and sometimes the unpleasant smell of both at the same time. The loud, rickety elevator creeps and pulls its way up to the third-floor opening to a large, bright, loftlike space. The hardwood floors and red brick walls give the space a warm, welcoming feeling, despite the high, warehouselike ceilings and expansive 2,000 square feet of space. There are numerous bright, colorfully painted banners promoting the organization's programs that line the walls—"Oakland Freedom Schools," "Leadership Excellence, Educating Youth for Social Change," "Drop Squad." The space feels so large probably because there are no walls, mostly cubicles that divide the employees' work spaces. The large windows welcome ample sunlight into each cubicle, where photographs of youth from past summer camps, school activities, or overnight retreats can be viewed.

Toward the rear of the building there is a meeting area labeled "The Spot," which serves as both a youth lounge and a conference room. There are brightly colored plastic stackable chairs; several red, green, and blue beanbags; and two covered couches, all circling a colorful rug in the center of the room. The four walls were carefully hand painted in a mural that depicts a story of youth challenges in Oakland, each wall with a different story that ends with a vibrant depiction of black youth rising up, breaking the chains that kept them down.

Around 3 o'clock, streams of young people flow into the office and provoke conversations with staff members. Any work that requires a computer needs to be completed by 3:00 because after that, the loud chatter and laughter of young people is usually too distracting for a focus on paperwork. Besides, the youth always find a way to use the staff's computers to log on to their MySpace pages. No one really minds this, of course. In fact, the youth are explicitly told by staff, "This is your space," which sometimes means that after 3:00 the office is filled with hip-hop music, blaring from small computer speakers. Around 4:00 the energy settles down, and youth work on homework or attend one of the after-school workshops held in The Spot.

Most of the young people at Leadership Excellence (LE) describe the organization as being a family. Perhaps this is because Nedra, my wife and the codirector of the organization, views our work as an extension of our own family. In fact, the young people refer to Nedra as "Mamma Ned" and often call me "Babba Shawn." My role, for the most part, is to build a sustainable organization; Nedra's job is to make sure that I do it in a way that does not jeopardize our integrity. In fact, Nedra and I debate, and sometimes argue, about which funding sources to pursue and how to use funds to expand LE's work. These debates are sometimes the material of an after-school discussion topic. I might say to the youth, "Okay, y'all, we can apply for a $100,000 grant but it will come from the Philip Morris Tobacco Company. Now let's discuss the pros and cons of this opportunity." Nedra might glare at me for raising the issue to the youth, but know that I am right to do so. Our arguments, debates, and disagreements are all from a place of love, respect, and care, which is perhaps why Mikayla and other young people describe LE as a family.

MIKAYLA AND MAMMA NED

Mikayla is a large girl with soft eyes and an old soul. Despite her cheerful spirit and youthful appearance, she has seen more than most 15-year-olds in Oakland, which probably explains why she is so self-confident. She was born in Tulare, California, and spent most of her early childhood years in Sacramento. At the age of 11, she moved to Oakland and has lived here ever since. Throughout Mikayla's life, her mother and her half-sister, Tatiana, have played prominent roles in shaping who she is today. She sees her mother as her best friend, and Tatiana, who is 9 years older than Mikayla, has been like a second mother to her. Mikayla's mother instilled in her the need to "speak your mind" and the need to be proactive, because "if you don't do it for yourself, nobody's going to do it for you."

Mikayla explains that being a part of LE is like being in a family. Her relationships with the adults, as well as the political education, have contributed to her activism:

> You can't describe it. It's like one of those heartfelt things that you have no words for because it's like my family. If anything ever happened to me or I needed somebody to talk to, I could always come here. I started coming to Leadership Excellence, my sister got me into it and I was shy, didn't say very much. Now I'm the person that always has something to say, and they made me think about a lot of political stuff that I wouldn't have thought of if I wasn't in the

program. They made me aware that I can make a change and act and not just accept things the way they are. It's kinda like . . . I'm in a family.

Since she can remember, Mikayla and her mother have never really had a home for a long period of time and frequently were homeless. This is largely because of her mother's substance abuse and alcoholism, which at times have required that Mikayla care for her mother. "Sometimes, she would just sleep all day and never get around to paying rent so we are always looking for a place to stay. Sometimes we would just sleep in our car, but when it gets too cold, I would have to call my sister, a friend, or somebody and ask them if we could stay with them."

Not having a stable place to live contributed to her lack of interest in school, which was exacerbated because she found the curriculum to be uninteresting and not applicable to her life. She explained that her teachers would routinely discriminate against her and other black students in her classes. For example, she had a teacher who gave all minority students grades of C or below. She also had teachers who believed that African Americans were lazy and didn't give needed help even though she asked for it. Consequently, she skipped a lot of school and eventually dropped out at the age of 15. She also often talks openly about racism she sees from the police. Mikayla dosen't trust teachers, police, or any authority figure. Most of her interactions with authority figures have been negative. For example, she witnessed police officers beating several of her friends directly in front of her.

The other day one of my friends, was being questioned by the police near my house. He was just standing there with his hands in his pockets, and the police officer was like, "Get your hands out of your pockets!" He said it twice. My friend told the officer, "Why do I have to get my hands out of my pockets, I'm just standing here watching what's going on." So the next thing I know, the police officer pulls out his gun and puts it to his neck and then puts it to his head. The officer said, "Uh . . . get your, get your hands out your pocket." So he pushed him up against the car, put handcuffs on him, broke his wrists in the scuffle! He was just standing there, with his hands in his pockets not doing anything!

Over time, encounters like this have eroded Mikayla's trust in police and, like many youth in Oakland, she has little faith or trust that the police will protect and serve her or that teachers care about her. Which is why

Mikayla came to LE, rather than the police, to share what she had seen on Saturday night.

Mikayla first became involved with LE at the age of 14. Tatiana, her older sister, who was studying social work, was an intern for LE and arranged for Mikayla to attend Camp Akili—one of the organization's summer programs. While Mikayla enjoyed the camp experience and the opportunity to get away from home, she also expressed that she felt like she had joined a supportive community of peers and adults where she could be herself and learn about social issues.

The close and supportive relationships Mikayla developed with staff and other youth at LE has had a tremendously positive impact on her life. She recalled a time when Nedra came to her house, without notice, after Mikayla had dropped out of school and stopped going to LE's programs. "Mamma Ned" is a 30-something, petite sistah-girl who speaks the truth and her mind with frank eloquence—a straight shooter, no room for bullshit. Her truth speaking has frequently made me, as her husband, nervous because I know that the truth is not always what folks want to hear. Somehow, however, her honesty is rarely misconstrued by others, and just like medicine, they might not want it, but her honesty is precisely what they need to hear. As with so many other relationships Nedra had developed over the years, she went further with Mikayla. Mikayla's absence prompted Nedra to speak to Mikayla's mother and visit Mikayla at her home unannounced. Mikayla commented:

> When Nedra popped up at my house, I did not expect her to be there. It was like the afternoon and I was still in my pajamas! She sat down with me and my mom and she told me that she was disappointed in me because I had dropped out of school. Now no one really ever said that to me before and it hit me hard! I didn't want to be a disappointment to anyone, especially Momma Ned, after all she had done for me! Nedra was saying that I needed to get back in school and I knew she was right. Sometimes it just takes the right person to tell you what you already know. So I got back in school and eventually graduated but I really felt that LE was there for me.

Mikayla has a great deal of respect for the young adult volunteers because LE offers so much comfort and support to her. For example, when she was homeless, she stayed with female volunteers or she sometimes would sleep in the LE office and use the showers at the YMCA a few blocks away. "If I hadn't been in Leadership Excellence, I would have never graduated from high school . . . I would probably have some kids or something like that." Mikayla feels a unique bond with other youth participants because they have all endured a lot of pain in their lives, and they have all supported her when she has needed them.

While care is formed by interpersonal connections, collective responsibility to improve community conditions is a common theme in LE's relationships with black youth. After Mikayla graduated from high school, Nedra hired her to help coordinate one of the organization's after-school youth-led programs. At 17, Mikayla is responsible for recruiting and organizing other youth to political awareness workshops on Saturday mornings.

> Having the ownership of the program makes me feel like I have a purpose for what was going on in the community. It gives me a sense of family and being a part of someplace where I could go where my ideas were respected. This never happens in school because I remember asking questions or I would say things in class at school and I was always shot down. But I feel that my ideas about how to improve the community, for example, are respected at LE. I feel really nurtured by everyone there.

Mikayla recalls one activity during a Saturday morning political education program where she learned a great deal about how to think and act in political ways:

> We were discussing a lot of issues that we [black youth] deal with here in Oakland. Typical stuff like crime, violence, drugs, police— stuff like that. Then we were asked, "If money was not an issue to address any of these issues what would you do?" I remember feeling like, are we ballin' or something like that? You know, the facilitator said that money is no object, we can do whatever we want to change the condition we want to take on in the community! It gave me a whole new way of thinking about stuff. There were no limits placed on who you are, where you are going, or what you want to do. So many things came out of that conversation because there were no limits placed on what we could imagine!

These rich conversations provided fertile ground for youth to develop a political understanding about juvenile justice, racism, poverty, and how these social issues shape their lives and communities. Through political education sessions, LE youth discuss the root causes of problems in their communities and strategize about how issues can be addressed. Collective responsibility to the broader black community is a critical component of LE's caring relationship with youth. Slogans such as "One life, one love, one people" or "I am because we are" and "I am my brother's/sister's keeper" are commonly found in newsletters and on T-shirts, which reinforce the idea of a common collective struggle. LE adults often say that one central purpose of the organization is to provide black youth with a "knowledge of self" in order for them to be better equipped to address social and community issues. Caring relationships are given meaning in collective struggle by creating a collective responsibility among black youth.

Mikayla finds meaning in relationships with adults at LE. These relationships help build optimism and hope. Despite what she witnessed on Saturday night being traumatic, there is a way to make it better. Such relationships, as Thompson observes, are driven by the urgency to "alert young people to the various threats to their survival and flourishing" (1995, p. 33), in order to carve pathways back to peace and well-being. As we sat on the couch, listening intensely to Mikayla, she continued to cry and explained that she wanted to go to the police but she was also fearful of what could happen to her, and perhaps her mother or sisters, if the perpetrator found out. We sat silently, without knowing exactly what to do or say. Lisa stood up from the couch and walked toward the door, turned around, and sat in a chair next to the couch. She brought her hands together and interlaced her fingers and, with a confused look, said, "Maybe I can call the police watch hotline. I can report it, but it would be anonymous." Mikayla looked up from staring at the floor. Her eyes were still moist. She said softly, "You think so?" While Lisa's call to the police never led to an arrest, the space for us to sit with her provided Mikayla a way to resolve what seemed to be an irreconcilable choice. Reflecting on that conversation, she commented, "They somehow don't make things seem like it's the end of the world when something happens, they make us feel like that there is always a way to make it better."

Mikayla's experiences with LE illustrates two points. First, trauma is not always conceptualized as a single tragic event, but can viewed as long-term exposure to dangerous situations, such as witnessing a murder. Sometimes trauma may stem from sociocultural environmental factors like distrust of the police and exposure to racist teachers or less obvious forms of trauma such as shame from being homeless and the psychic energy required to hide it from peers. For Mikayla, these experiences exact a toll on her overall well-being. Second, relationships among black youth in urban communities requires that adults transgress the traditional boundaries of trust between individuals by placing collective responsibility at the center of meaningful relationships. "We need to do whatever is possible to support youth with self-transformation," Nedra asserts frequently in staff meetings. "These relationships make us more than another after-school program because when I say to our youth, 'I know your grandmother or your momma,' they respect that I can say it and mean it; I really know their personal struggles. I think this gives us more trust because we are like extended family to these young folks."

These close relationships, however, are not without challenges. I recall a difficult group session that I was leading with both youth and adult volunteers. During that time in my life, I was having difficulty balancing care of my newborn child, raising money for LE, and transitioning to a new career as an assistant professor. As a result of these personal pressures, I could not focus on the training that I was conducting. I was unaware that many of the youth in the group had noticed my level of stress when one young person asked me, "What's wrong?" Until that point, I believed that my role as an adult community leader, founder, and executive director was to be a role model to young people by showing them a "trouble free" adult. In response to her question, I immediately put on the adult, "problem free" face and responded that there was nothing wrong with me. After they continued to probe me about why I seemed so stressed out, I finally confessed my troubles. I began describing my fears of not having raised enough money to keep the doors open. I told them how these financial issues would affect my family and new child. I also expressed my thoughts about leaving the organization altogether. After my emotional confession to the group, I was concerned that I had transgressed the boundaries of the adult professional role by violating the unspoken rule that you should separate your personal life from professional activities, but to my surprise, several youth responded, "Hey, man, you got problems just like me!" or "I thought you had life all figured out, that's cool that you got issues to deal with." Redefining my role as an adult partner contributed to an unanticipated outcome: I learned that when I made myself vulnerable, the young people could support me by listening just as I had listened to them. My vulnerability actually deepened their respect for me because I was honest with them about something as important as my own life. I am not advocating that all youth development professionals make their personal lives available to the young people with whom they work. The lesson I draw from this experience is that trust is also a collective phenomenon and as we care for youth in moments of our own vulnerability, they care for us as well.

KEVIN'S REBOUND

While vulnerability is sometimes scary, risky, and uncomfortable, it frequently is a pathway to strong and meaningful relationships with young people. Perhaps no one knows this better than Kevin, a 20-year-old brotha with shoulder-length red-tinted locks who is constantly being torn between life in the streets and peace of mind. It is not his fake gold front teeth, baggy pants, and white T-shirt that have earned him respect in his East Oakland neighborhood, but rather his charisma, style, and intelligence. Kevin's sister had become concerned about his involvement in drug sales, crime, and petty theft, and that led her to call LE and inquire about how we could support Kevin. "I was falling really deep into the streets and digging a hole that I knew I could not get out! I felt like I was trapped and stuck getting deeper and deeper into the streets." Kevin grew up in East Oakland and as a child would look up to the older teens on his block. He was enamored by the "O.G.s" (original gangsters) on his block and saw them as strong male role models:

> When I was younger, the O.G.s would be out there on the block holdin' down. They would look like strong, powerful men. I grew up without a father and was raised by my grandma, my momma, and my sister. As I grew up, I felt like I needed to be around some men. I started hanging out with them because I need to learn how to be a man. When I was 14 or 15, I started to notice their nice cars and they always had money and girls with them. So I was like, "How can I get like that?" I remember when I would ask them for a dollar, and they would give me 5 or 10. As a youngster that's a lot of money!

Like many young men in Oakland, Kevin wanted only the glamour of street life, not the danger. In fact, he admitted that when he started hanging out, he didn't really know that violence, running from the police, and watching over your back was a part of selling drugs. Shortly after he began to hang out with groups of older teens, he experienced firsthand the danger that comes with selling drugs. He recalled the first time he held a gun, that "it was heavier than I thought it would be," but he quickly got used to wearing baggy clothing to conceal the gun when he needed to carry it.

> My niggas was always out on the block selling, grinding, trying to make some money. I had to really earn my respect with everyone. I don't want to go into detail about what I did but I had to do a lot and go through a lot. It was like an initiation, a fraternity or something. But when I got in, it was like no turning back! I just focused my mind and molded myself into a gangsta.

But gangsta life turned out to be a tragedy for Kevin. He and his best friend, Amir, would often go to parties in East Oakland and shout out the name of their block, seeking respect and perhaps recognition from other folks at the party.

The night of May 8, 2004, began like any other Saturday night. Kevin gathered with his friends and heard about a party in nearby Richmond. As at many other parties, there was plenty to smoke and drink. They weren't really concerned that the party was on another turf. Kevin commented about hanging out with his friends: "When we all get together, we really don't give a fuck about anything!" When the young lady who invited them told them to "stay inside and keep the door closed because the niggas in Richmond don't like cats from Oakland," they really didn't pay her much attention. During the party, it wasn't long before other guys from the neighborhood attempted to crash the party and were quickly turned away by the host. Later that night, after everyone had left, Kevin was playing dominoes in the kitchen. The apartment was small and hot so his friend Amir kept opening the door to cool off. Amir had taken off his shirt and was standing in the open door when he was hit with bullets.

> All I heard were the gunshots outside—*bap, bap, bap, bap* . . . My first thought was, Are they trying to scare us or something? So I just kept on playing dominoes. When I looked up, Amir came running into the house. As he ran in, I could tell something scared him because he scanned the room and looked around for someone, and then he ran straight to me. As he came to me, I grabbed him and I looked down and saw all the blood. That's when I knew he had been shot. I was shocked and I didn't know what to do! What was I suppose to do? We called the ambulance and they came about 30 to 45 minutes after we called. During this time, Amir was laying on the floor trying so hard to live. His eyes were still wide open, but he was grunting and trying to hold on. When the ambulance arrived, one nurse put her gloves on and put her finger in one of the bullet holes, I guess to try to stop the bleeding. Blood was everywhere, man. As she was trying to stop his bleeding, I remember this clearly, the police rushed in the door and grabbed everybody including the nurse and pushed all of us into the back room! As I turned around to look back at Amir, I saw him panic because his chest was going in and out real fast. The police started to snap pictures of him, you know, homicide pictures of his body, but he was still alive!

The trauma of witnessing what had occurred to his friend Amir was more than Kevin could take. Anger, rage, sadness, and confusion all swirled inside of him with no place to go.

I started trippin' out—I cannot even describe what I felt, it's something you gotta experience for yourself to understand, so I blew up
with rage. They arrested everyone but took me to jail because I
didn't have any identification. I remember just sitting there thinking, Is he dead or alive? I sort of knew he was dead.

Oftentimes traumatic events like the one Kevin experienced go undi-
agnosed and ultimately contribute to even greater distrust, resentment, and
anger. After spending 2 days in jail, Kevin learned that he was a suspect in
the murder of his own best friend! Despite the fact that there was no evidence to suggest that he should be a suspect, he now has a permanent
record that indicates that he was a suspect in a murder investigation. Without his having a meaningful and productive outlet to describe and heal from
what happened, Kevin's frustration and anger turned into numbness.

I try to put that shit behind me but every time I go and try to get a
job, that "suspect to murder" pops up even though I had nothing to
do with it. Everytime it happens, it reminds me of the whole ordeal
again. It pisses me off because it reminds me of what the police
did, you know how they flipped his body over and took homicide
pictures of him when he was still alive! I just didn't feel anything,
I just felt numb. I just felt stuck in the middle. I didn't feel good
about anything, or bad. I just felt stuck and I didn't give a fuck
about anything!

Events such as these often result in unresolved rage, aggression, depression, and fatalism (Poussaint & Alexander, 2000). Few educational and
youth development researchers have considered the ways in which trauma
shapes both the educational and youth development experiences (Obidah,
et al., 2004). Traumatic events like the one Kevin experienced have an impact on individual well-being, but there are also social, political, and moral
implications that reverberate throughout the broader community. Amir
was a son, a brother, and a uncle, whose loss will be mourned by those
who knew him, but mostly ignored in the media. Local concerns about
safety and crime will continue to shape home values and thus educational
quality in neighborhoods and residents will demand that their milquetoast
leaders provide greater safety. More important, however, are the existential questions Kevin and others will struggle with in trying to make meaning out of profound loss. Unfortunately, these forms of trauma have become
normalized, perversely usual, in black urban communities where death and
dying have become so common that some youth tell their teachers what
they want to wear to their own funerals.

Violence of this sort poses a serious threat to social bonds, relationships, belonging, and sense of purpose. West suggests that the most profound result of violence is a "numbing detachment from others and a self-destructive disposition toward the world" (1993, p. 14). The impact of violence in communities has led many researchers to reframe how they look at violence, moving away from restrictive beliefs about maladaptive behavior toward a more broad conceptualization that considers the ecological terrain (the social, economic, political, and cultural environment) in which violence occurs (Brooks-Gunn et al., 1993; Garbarino, 1995; Garbarino & Abramowitz, 1992). While there is substantial evidence to suggest that "violence destroys the underlying interrelatedness and interdependence not only of its perpetrators and victims, but of the community at large" (Ward, 1995, p. 4), we understand very little about the redemptive process that restores these mutual ties and relationships. Restoring relationships, trust, care, and hope contributes to the healing process and is an important precondition for social action (Piven & Cloward, 1979).

In Johnson's examination of black youths grappling with death in a classroom setting, she argues for the need to "make connections between the day-to-day realities of students' lives and the day-to-day process of teaching and learning that takes place in urban public schools across the United States" (1995, p. 217). After realizing the profound impact of homicide on the lives of young people in her community, she came to understand the ways in which social marginalization and oppression create and sustain urban trauma. In connecting students' real-life experiences to classroom practices she describes a healing process that integrates issues of power, history, self-identity, and the possibility of collective agency and struggle.

ENACTING RADICAL CARE

Traditional modes of care in black communities have always been central to sustaining black life and affirming black identity in the context of brutal racism. Without these modes of care, hope, possibility and meaning give way to profound meaninglessness and hopelessness, which pose a serious threat to black life. These modes of care function as buffers, as cultural armor, that have created and sustained community life and "ways of life and struggle that embodied values of service and sacrifice, love and care, discipline and excellence" (West, 1993, p. 15). Such views of care were defined not simply by compassion, but also by communal survival: community members would support one another through personal hardships such as death, illness, or lack of shelter. There are few community spaces,

however, for black youth to heal from the type of trauma experienced by
Mikayla and Kevin. Schools are ill prepared to engage young people in a
healing process. Often schools actually *breed* violence through draconian
rules and a fetish for control, containment, and punishment. Churches often
are overly resistant to urban black youth culture. After years of trial and
error, we learned at LE that youth rarely want or need to be talked at, but
want to be listened to without judgment, which of course is very difficult
when you deeply care about someone.

Amir's death occurred shortly after Kevin started hanging out at the
LE youth center. Fortunately he had a community of caring adults, peers,
and what Noguera calls a "humane environment" in which to talk about
the incident and there was a process that allowed him to openly grieve,
heal, and hope again for a better way of life. After about a month, he was
given a part-time administrative job sorting mail, copying, and running
errands for the staff. In 2001, I stepped down from the executive director
position, because of my other demands at the university, and Dereca Blackmon, a 30-something, Stanford-educated, gritty, streetwise sistah, took the
helm of the agency in June 2002. For some reason, Dereca immediately
bonded with Kevin and took it upon herself to support him through his
healing process.

Dereca explained, "I am always drawn to the most challenging young
people, the ones that everyone else cannot, or will not, deal with." Kevin
was no exception; he had dropped out of high school a couple of years
before he came to LE. When young people walk into Dereca's office at LE,
she is always happy to see them and welcomes them with a hug and smile.
In fact, hugging and embracing is an important ritual in LE's culture. Dereca
explains:

> I am always excited to see the young folks come in. Good to see you
> man . . . howz you momma? We are all excited; we hug them and
> give them much love. Where else are they going to get that feeling
> of belonging, like really being honored for just walking through the
> door? Where else are they going to get that feeling of being cele-
> brated for just being who they are? You don't get it at home, not at
> school, not on the streets, really. And they so much want that good
> feelin'. Like Neal, he is rejected everywhere else, but here he's a
> legend! Where else do youth get to feel like a legend!

Neal is a young man who had been an outcast in so many places not
only because he is openly gay, but also because of his appearance. He is
tall, with light skin, bright red hair, and freckles. Despite his being ridi-
culed everywhere else, the young people in LE saw him as a part of the

family. This was reinforced by staff, who celebrated Neal when he would show up to programs after school, because of his outlandish personality and vibrant energy. Neal, and all youth, are always greeted with a hug. This is largely because central to the organizational philosophy is that black youth are rarely embraced by adults, or by one another, in ways that convey care, compassion, and love. In the harsh reality of urban life, tough fronts and postures are required to navigate violence and potentially life-threatening situations (Dance, 2002). These postures, however, are also walls that inhibit the healing process, and when young people embrace each other the tough exteriors melt away and the youth can be at ease. It is through touch and embrace that deep and meaningful relationships begin with connections from the soul.

More important than a single embrace, however, was the caring environment fostered at LE. Kevin started participating in a black male support group called Brotha's Keeper, where 10–15 young men from 14 to 25 years old would meet every Thursday night to talk about issues ranging from loss to academic success. The support group gave Kevin an opportunity to grapple with not only the loss of Amir but also the rage and numbness Kevin was experiencing. Connecting to other youth and young adults who experienced similar trauma provided Kevin a rare space in which to heal. He commented:

> The only way I would deal with this stuff before I came here was to drink. But that would make me real evil. All the rage would just come out to such an extent that my partners would tell me I need to stop drinking. I really didn't know how to deal with this trauma. I don't know about getting a psychologist or something like that, cuz if I go see a psychologist, how they gone tell me 'bout something they never been through. The group of brotha's really helped me see what happened and deal with it differently. We talked about all types of little things that would keep my mind off of the streets. One time I got up and told a story about what happened, with Amir. The energy in the room was cool so everybody in the room was getting up to tell their stories so I kinda got a chance to let out some of my emotions. Everybody was emotional, so you know what I'm saying? I got to tell my story and just based off the energy in the room, I got a chance to let out my feelings.

These types of experiences were critical to Kevin's healing process. By being in a safe environment, he felt safe enough to listen to other young men's stories but also he felt the security to share his own. These environments are not easy to create. In fact, many of the young men had come from rival turfs. The leader of the young men's group, however, had taken time to prepare each participant by taking him away on a retreat to build a sense of trust and community. The investment in time and energy during the retreat created trust and respect whereby young people could be vulnerable to openly share.

Every day when Kevin entered the office, he would check in with Dereca to have a casual conversation or to get her advice about something. Dereca commented, "I would always check in with Kevin and say, What's up? We just talk about stuff, going on in his family, or on his block, his future or whatever." If he missed a day or so, she would ask him, "Why weren't you here yesterday, where were you?" She might add, "We missed you; we needed you to help set up the room for the meeting." For Kevin, the environment was a welcome change from what he experienced on the streets. On the block, he always had to be suspicious of everyone's actions.

Kevin developed a greater sense of belonging and connection, to Dereca and to the entire LE community of adults and other youth. He stated, "The people here trust me with everything, I feel like it is another kind of family because I feel like I belong here."

On one occasion, the young people decided that they wanted to paint a mural in the youth section of the office and had contacted a well-known local artist to train the youth in how to paint a mural and to work with them to create a mural that would convey the values and principles of the LE community. Kevin worked with the artist, K-Dub, for hours on the mural. His hard work was rewarded when K-Dub painted a portrait of Kevin, in the center of the mural, to represent a positive image of black male youth in the city. When K-Dub included Kevin in the mural, it also transformed how Kevin began to see himself. Kevin declared, "Man, the mural really made me feel like I was significant around here, like I mattered."

Belonging to the LE community was an important part of Kevin's healing process. His connections with other youth and young adults who shared a common experience provided powerful bonds that led to new, positive forms of community life. These strong, rich community connections are highly political. Ward argued that "the parenting of a black child is a political act. The psychological survival of a Black child largely depends on the Black family's ability to endure racial and economic discrimination and to negotiate conflicting and multiple roles and demands" (2000, p. 51). Similarly, relationships with youth are strengthened by honest and sometimes harsh discussions with adults about the conditions of black people. Building critical consciousness, or the capacity to understand how social, systemic, and structural issues shape day-to-day life, is an important component in building caring relationships. These conversations force young people to confront their own responsibilities as well as understand how to confront racial and economic oppression. These conversations are pivotal in moving from beliefs about care as simply compassion, to more radical ideas about care that foster critical consciousness and encourage changes in behavior. Kevin recalls one conversation he had with Dereca that illustrates this point:

> I'll never forget what she told me. I remember she said that basically what we want to do while y'all are here at LE is tell you that you have been lied to by society. What we see out there in the streets is not the truth. But we think that all there is to life is the block and partying. But she said that was what society wanted us to do, keep us docile slaves or whatever so they could do whatever they want to our communities, sell us stuff that's not good for us. All the while, we're just blind to everything going on. No one ever said anything to me before like that. So that's what really started making me real close to Dereca.

These conversations are significant because they not only establish care between two people, but also signify a broader caring about the well-being of black people. It is in this context that care is both intimate and political, individual and communal. Care, in this sense, allows young people to see themselves in a broader context of justice and liberation. Dereca noted, "We care about youth, because we love black people; and because we love black people, we care so much about youth." This mutual understanding and expectation that care, love, and well-being are intimately tied to achieving justice and liberation deepens the relationships between adults and among youth at LE. Dereca gave an example:

> One day Kevin found a way to go to the roof of the building at LE and he was feeding some birds bread. I guess someone saw him up there and called the police and told the police that a black man was going to jump from the building or something. Next thing I know there are five police cars out front; 10 police officers rush into the office asking how to get to the roof because there is a dangerous man up there. I calmly told them that he was a youth in our program and was on the roof feeding the birds. They demanded to go to the rooftop, but I went with them cuz I knew they would probably beat Kevin's ass if I was not there watching them.

Dereca's actions signified care about Kevin as an individual young person; further, it prompted a more radical form of care that was informed by a political awareness of how police treated black males in Oakland. This

required that she use her adult authority to intervene and buffer any problems that might ensue from Kevin being another target for Oakland police.
Care as a political act conveys the idea that individuals belong to a broader
community, and any threat to the individual is a threat to the community.
The strong sense of belonging, coupled with a radical form of caring, a form
that is both personal and political, creates a fabric of trust and expectation
that foster a sense of common struggle among youth and adults. Radical care
can be seen everywhere in the organization. LE's slogans, such as "One life,
one love, one people"; "I am because we are"; and "I am my brother's/sister's
keeper," reinforce the idea of collective struggle. LE adults often say that one
central purpose of the organization is to provide black youth with a "knowledge of self" in order for them to be better equipped to address social and
community issues. By creating a collective black youth identity that is connected to politically charged issues in Oakland, black youth develop politicized racial identities. Gregory noted that collective identities are
"formed and reformed through struggles in which the 'winning of identification,' the articulation of collective needs, interests, and commitments is
itself a key stake in the exercise of domination and resistance" (1998, p. 18).

THE SOFT SIDE OF REVOLUTION, CARE, AND REBUILDING COMMUNITY LIFE

Care is facilitated by building critical consciousness among black youth
and providing opportunities and space for political expression and engagement. For example, ongoing police misconduct in Oakland in March
2003 prompted the chief of police, the mayor, and a local congresswoman
to convene a town hall meeting to learn more about the community's experience with police misconduct. Dereca was asked to attend to represent
Oakland's youth. Upon arriving at the meeting, she realized that no young
people had been invited and believed that it was important for the officials to hear from youth themselves. She called from her cell phone several LE participants and asked them to come down to City Hall and tell
them what was happening with black youth in Oakland.

> When I got to the meeting, it was the usual cast of characters, the
> mayor, congresswoman Barbara Lee, and the chief of police. We
> were there to talk about youth but there were no youth at the table.
> So I called a few youth who were hanging out at the LE center and
> asked them to come and represent and speak their mind to these
> so-called leaders. When they arrived, they got on the open mic and
> blew everyone away.

When Kevin approached the microphone, everyone immediately focused on how he dressed. His baggy jeans, oversized "hoody" sweatshirt, tennis shoes, and shoulder-length locks seemed to typify the urban uniform for young black males in Oakland. Although this style of dress is common among urban youth, black young males who dress in this way are often labeled as thugs and troublemakers by the police and often targeted for surveillance and searches. Kevin commented about his experience with the police:

> I just want to be real with y'all. When I am out there I feel like a target for the police. People see me, and look at the way I dress, and treat me like less than a man, less than human! I feel like a target for self-destruction! Sometimes I feel like giving up, fuck it! But I am a wise person, you cannot judge me by the way I look because I know what wisdom is inside me and I just need the opportunity for you to see me for who I am.

By providing meaningful opportunities to give voice to black youth and articulate their feelings about the police, LE challenges the problem-driven discourse about black youth in public policy and recasts black youth as key civic partners in community-change efforts. Equally important is the mutual trust that developed between Dereca and Kevin. Because LE creates a space in which black youth can be heard, and recasts black youth as political actors, Kevin pushed himself to live up to the positive political expectation that LE staff holds of him.

> They [LE adults] see stuff that you don't see in yourself, and they try to bring it out of you. They see me as an activist or something, and I'm not political like that. But when Dereca lets me speak my mind to folks like the mayor and political people, it makes you want to live up to that image, you know.

Care is created between LE youth and adults through mutual trust and reciprocity. That is, the adults have the expectation that black youth will engage in political affairs, and in turn black youth conceptualize civic and community change as a responsibility. By creating forums, participating in campaigns for youth funding, and other civic activities, LE challenges politically disabling discourse about black youth in Oakland as a threat to neighborhood safety. Care is created and sustained through opportunities in which black youth are viewed as legitimate political actors. The expectation that LE adults have about black youth reconstitutes images of black youth, no longer seen as a civic problem but as community activists, and

LE youth reciprocate by viewing community engagement as a responsibility. Care also involves creating a collective racial and cultural identity among black youth that provides them with a unified understanding of their plight in American society. This is important, given the entrenched ways in which black youth in urban communities have been socialized to view each other through fragmented, often adversarial neighborhood identities (East Oakland versus West Oakland). LE's strategy to create a unified racial identity among black youth helps them develop identities that mitigate neighborhood turf conflicts.

The rich and meaningful relationships Kevin had developed at LE had contributed to new consciousness about his own life and gave him a sense of purpose. The meeting at City Hall Kevin had attended was broadcast on C-SPAN and was seen by thousands of people throughout the country. After learning about the significance of his comments and his newfound activist identity, Kevin became more eager to learn all he could so that he could be a better advocate for other black youth in Oakland. But he had not completed high school and never received his GED. Dereca had been nudging Kevin to enroll in a program, but her constant encouragement to get his GED only reminded him of what he had not accomplished.

Dereca continued to push him about his future plans. Despite being deeply committed to social justice, and having begun to organize his own block, he still had not completed school. She told him that he had to get his GED; everything he was doing was good, but without his education, he eventually would turn back to the streets. Kevin never did well in school, nor did he really see the need to get his GED, which made their conversation tense. Shortly after, Kevin stopped coming to work. He stopped participating in the programs and disappeared from the LE community entirely. Dereca feared that she had pushed him away by pressing him so hard about getting his GED. She lamented:

> He just stopped coming to work. I didn't see or hear from Kevin in nearly 3 months. This is after talking to him almost every day. I was hysterical, asking everyone if they know what was going on with him. I didn't know if he was alive or what. I talked to some of his friends here and they told me that they see him sometimes but he seemed distant, and he really didn't have much to say to them. What did I say to push him away? Why didn't he call or come around? Deep inside I was tore up because I knew I had pushed him away. After about 3 months, I was sitting right here at my desk in my office and he just showed up out of nowhere. I just burst into tears when I saw him. I asked, "Where have you been? Why didn't you call? What is going on with you?" I cried and hugged him even

though I was so upset. He said to me, "I thought a lot about what you said and I wanted to do more with my life." He pulled out a picture of himself in his graduation cap holding his GED diploma and said, "Look, it's me!" I just cried and I still have the picture. He had been going to school the entire time, working on his GED. Then he told me, "And I also got my driver's license." We hugged and cried together. Then I hit him and told him, "Don't you ever do that to me again—you could have called me and told me what you were doing."

Janelle Dance (2002) encourages us to think more seriously about what she calls "the power of humane investments," the investments in young people's lives that require that we see in them more than they see in themselves. These investments build relationships that raise expectations about the possibilities in young people's lives. Dereca's investments in Kevin and Nedra's investment in Mikayla illustrate that one of the first steps in the healing process is to care more radically about black youth. This means that we ask not so much what we can do for black youth, but more important, how relationships can recalibrate what black youth can do for themselves.

One of the undertheorized aspects of social capital is the conceptualization of hope and its impact on community, educational, and civic life among black youth. Both Mikayla and Kevin demonstrate the ways in which radical care departs from traditional ideas about care by placing a greater focus on the impact of trauma and the collective process required to heal from it. By focusing on relationships and dimensions of community change, radical care serves as an important community and social resource for youth. Care is facilitated by intergenerational advocacy that challenges negative concepts about black youth and is developed by building a collective racial and cultural identity and sustained by understanding personal challenges as political issues. Healthy relationships are fundamental prerequisites for radical care between youth and adults. If care is given meaning through relationships between individuals, radical care is formed in community.

3

Building a Healing Community

Then they all gathered around Sonny and Sonny played. Every now and again one of them seemed to say, amen. Sonny's fingers filled the air with life, his life. But that life contained so many others. . . . Freedom lurked around us and I understood, at last, that he could help us be free if we would listen, that he would never be free until we did.

—James Baldwin, *Sonny's Blues*

HEALING IS A DANCE between the individual and the community. For black youth, this dance is both intensely personal and profoundly communal, and without relationships and connections the healing process is rendered inert. Community has served as safe sanctuaries from the "trauma of racism and oppression" (Stevens, 2002) in the black experience. Forming community is more than living on the same block, participating in neighborhood meetings, and knowing your neighbors. In black culture, community is about fostering hope and justice. Community can be an important buffer against trauma and can promote the healing necessary for activism.

Camp Akili is a 5-day summer camp where African American teens can continue the healing process and nurture their political consciousness about social and community issues. Such spaces are not new to the black experience. Historically, they have sustained black life in the form of *quilombos*, maroon communities where Africans could physically, emotionally, and spiritually resist the brutality of slavery. Churches in many ways have also provided a libratory space for communities to retreat from the hostilities of racial oppression and resist domination (Mattis, 1997; Mattis & Jagers, 2001). Similarly, healing communities have traditionally

77

formed the basis of rites-of-passage ceremonies in some West African communities.

For years, community organizers, activists, and youth development practitioners have recognized that forming and building community is much more than bringing people together around a common purpose. Rather, community building involves fostering a collective spirit and developing a keen awareness of the interrelatedness of community members. Social movement scholars have attempted to grapple with the theoretical significance of community building in collective action. These scholars focus on the interpsychological and intracommunal forces that compel groups of people to act on behalf of the common good (Fantasia, 1988; Klandermans, 1984; Melucci, 1988).

Over the past decade, researchers have employed a social capital framework to better understand how personal networks and relationships translate to a desired outcome. This research has focused on the prerequisites for collective action, community mobilization, and community building (Fuchs, Shapiro, & Minnite, 2001; Putnam, 1993; Saegert, Thompson, & Warren, 2001). While the social capital framework is important to our understanding of how networks and relationships bind people together, it is a different concept from that of community. Formulations of social capital are broadly defined as "features of social organization, such as networks, norms, and trust, that facilitate coordination and cooperation for mutual benefit" (Putnam, 1993, p. 36). That is, as individuals extend their relationships with other individuals, institutions, or groups, they are more likely to have greater access to resources such as jobs, educational opportunities, and neighborhood safety (Fuchs, Shapiro, & Minnite, 2001; Portes, 1998).

Community, on the other hand, is more than networked relationships, trust, and mutual expectations. Community is a consciousness of the interrelatedness one has with others. This conceptualization of community is rooted in political, cultural, and economic histories as well as contemporary struggles in which people collectively act to make meaning of their social condition. Communities are created when people share a collective consciousness about their history, neighborhoods, racial and ethnic identities, gender, politics, and geography and act to defend, rebuild, or resist threats to that collective understanding. Through our consciousness and action we form communities in which healing and activism come together.

For black youth, these types of communities are rare, yet vitally important, given the turmoil in many urban neighborhoods. They are important because they provide young people with a space for honest reflection and painful reconciliation and offer meaning making about their conditions. Sometimes these communities are formed and maintained on basketball courts through casual conversations or in barber shop conversations or on porches while hair is being braided. These spaces are created out of a need for black youth to share, testify, and heal.

REFRAMING COMMUNITY AND CIVIC LIFE

There are at least two points of entry into this notion of community building. The first is black womanist scholars, such as Patricia Hill-Collins, Audre Lourde, bell hooks, and Alice Walker, who provide a framework to critique and deconstruct the ways in which patriarchal white supremacy and homophobia are woven into the fabric of Western epistemology and sustained in the structural realities of American society. Perhaps one of the most significant contributions of the black womanist intellectual tradition is the ways in which privilege is made visible; another is the uncovering of the complex ways in which the intersections of identity resist forms of domination. In the face of white supremacy and patriarchy, communities emerge for both protection and resistance from these forms of domination.

While domination is often conceptualized as structural barriers to economic mobility, or unearned and invisible group advantages, domination (white supremacy, patriarchy, classism) also threaten the existential well-being and the collective consciousness necessary for resisting and confronting painful experiences. bell hooks reminds us that white supremacy, racism, and sexism do not manifest themselves only in material ways; they affect our psychological well-being: "Black people are wounded in our hearts, minds, bodies, and spirits" (1993, p. 11).

There are spaces of refuge that are often hidden from public view that allow African American youth to reconcile, confront, and heal from psychic wounds. However, these spaces are often misunderstood and grossly undertheorized. Healthy community-building allows for black youth to remove the masks and tough exteriors they need to survive and encourages them to share their problems, hopes, and dreams. Building these radical communities requires us to understand how black youth care, love, dream, imagine, and hope. Through testimony, dialogue, and witnessing, we can understand an affirming love for humanity and justice.

As Somé (1999) argues, the purpose of community is to nurture and protect the individual, because it is the sum total of all individuals' purpose, dreams, and talents that creates community. The individual, knowing his or her purpose, will then invest energy in sustaining the community. "There is a certain reciprocity at work here, because the community recognizes [that] its own vitality is based in the support and protection of each of its individuals. . . . The individuals, knowing this, in turn delivers [*sic*] to the community" the gifts, talents, and dreams the community has inspired in them (p. 34).

Camp Akili is a community of possibilities for black youth. At the camp, set in the tranquil California mountains, they develop new visions for their lives, their communities, and our society. Youth from urban communities, juvenile hall, county probation, churches, and after-school programs come to unlearn the damaging messages given to them by society, rediscover their true selves, and rebuild their identities in a way that inspires justice and activism.

This chapter explores one approach to building and sustaining community life among black youth. Through detailed ethnography of this 5-day summer camp, I examine how trust, relationship building, and political consciousness form the basis for profound community where healing occurs. I argue that our understanding of community among black youth must consider how the healing process contributes to more radical forms of civic life. This chapter provides a more nuanced understanding of how black youth assign meaning to their social condition and develop political consciousness about community and social issues during this summer program.

CAMP AKILI: A PEDAGOGY OF RADICAL HEALING AND CARE

Camp Akili was created in 1989 to build a community where African American youth could heal from the trauma of institutional and internalized oppression. The camp was designed to force participants to think critically about various social issues and provide a structural framework in which to better understand oppression. Over an intense 5 days of activities, discussions, and workshops, approximately 100 young people learn about the root causes of certain social problems and learn to take on leadership roles in their communities. The camp uses dynamic, interactive workshops that encourage participants to dialogue about the painful experiences with racism, violence, and loss and creates an environment where youth can be open and reflect on their lives, communities, and personal struggles. Heavy dosages of black culture, political consciousness, and love form the basis for the camp's community. Chants such as "Say it loud, I'm black and I'm proud" or T-shirts that say, "One life, one love, one people" communicate to youth that they are all members of a loving black community.

Youth who attend Camp Akili come from local high schools, community-based organizations, churches, and county probation offices in the Bay Area that refer teens to the program. Participants complete an application for participation in camp and are selected by (1) level of need for positive interaction with peers and adults, (2) income and family size, (3) level of community participation, (4) level of commitment to remain in the program. The goal of the selection process is to select a wide range of students who come from a variety of social, educational, and class backgrounds. Leadership Excellence believes that a diverse clientele creates a richer and more meaningful learning environment because teens learn best when they are not given labels such as "at risk," "gifted," or "troubled."

The camp's goals are threefold: to provide structured activities that develop and enhance political awareness, to provide participants with opportunities that encourage and promote psychological and physical wellness, and to provide hands-on experiences that are intended to stimulate learning about activism and leadership. At the camp, each young person is assigned to a "village," which is a discussion group consisting of up to 10 teen participants. Trained college students and young adult volunteer counselors lead group discussions about community and youth issues such racism, avoiding violence, and sexual responsibility. These discussions are significant opportunities for youth to dialogue about issues in the safety of smaller group settings. The camp uses a sequence of structured activities that begins with an experiential activity, then moves to small-group discussion, then ends with a large community discussion of how the lessons or ideas can be applied to oneself or one's community. Dereca Blackmon, the executive director of Leadership Excellence, described how community is formed in Camp Akili:

> The camp provides a broad variety of support for African American youth by first and foremost building relationships with them, positive relationships, between the youth and each other, and also the youth and healthy adults. So I think that relationship aspect, I think we probably do better than anybody else. We do that through experiential workshops that give us a chance to really share with each other and address some of the pain that young people are experiencing in their lives via systems of oppression. We create the opportunities for them to express that pain that they've experienced via racism, sexism, violence, and some of the things that they are experiencing in their lives. Through these opportunities, we mentor them, we support them, we give them hugs, we love them through that process of looking at some of the core issues that cause the pain in the first place. In addition, we provide them with a political education to contextualize the pain that they've experienced. So it's like, they know they are in pain and they know it's not right, but we provide them with the political education to give them that context to see. I think that there is an ah-ha moment which is really important to them as well.

Youth are exposed to a series of powerful experiential activities that force them to connect their personal struggles to broad social and political issues. Each day of the camp is progressively more intense. On the 1st day all the activities and discussions focus on self-awareness. Many of the activities involve group trust building in which youth share stories but also participate in activities and games where they physically touch one another. This is significant because an important aspect of building community in Camp Akili involves moving past the fragile exteriors that youth bring with them. Touch such as a handshake, back rub, high five, or hug can establish connections between young people in a way that erodes the masks some young people wear to protect themselves from being hurt.

The 2nd day focuses on violence and provides youth opportunities to explore the impact of violence, loss, and fear in their lives. The 3rd day of the camp explores racism and focuses on building healthy racial identity. The day is filled with activities that force young people to question what it means to be black and is structured on conversations about racial oppression. These activities might include understanding the significance of the terms "good hair" and "bad hair" or why people use the term "nigga." The 3rd day ends with a powerful experiential visualization in order to re-create the experiences of Africans being sold into slavery.

The 4th day of the camp confronts sexism and is often the most emotional day of the camp, because youth share their stories of pain regarding sexual abuse. The 5th day is designed to prepare the campers to return to their communities and confront obstacles they will encounter. The camp ends with an activity in which each participant must climb a 30-foot wall. The wall represents challenges they will face that appear to be insurmountable upon leaving camp. The activity illustrates that with the support of their new community, they can overcome even the most difficult challenges in life. At first, everyone laughs and doesn't believe that it can be done. But one person at a time, with people pulling from the top and pushing from the bottom, and everyone cheering along the way, everyone gets over the wall.

CAMP AKILI FROM TERELL'S POINT OF VIEW

When his phone rang at 3:00 a.m., Terell, a 16-year-old from Oakland, had a feeling that bad news would soon follow. "We got that fool Kev," an excited voice said on the other end. "What you mean?" Terell asked. "We shot him, Terell, he won't be coming at us no more." Two weeks ago Terell had got into a fight with someone from a different neighborhood. The fight came about as a result of Lil J accusing Terell of snitching to the police. Angry at the accusation, Terell confronted Lil J at a party and told him to stop spreading the rumor. Refusing to back down, Lil J fought Terell. In fact, the two had fought on at least two other occasions for the same reason. Terell knew he had to quash the issue with Lil J because if they kept fighting, the situation could escalate to something much worse.

Lil J happened to be at a house party on Saturday night, and Terell, on his own initiative, took the opportunity to approach Lil J to end the squabble. They talked and smoothed out their misunderstanding and ended the ongoing battle. Feeling good about ending the squabble, Terell left the party. About an hour later Terell's crew arrived, unaware that Lil J and Terell had agreed upon a truce. Terell's crew confronted Lil J, who was confused because he thought that the issue was resolved. Unfortunately, Lil J was shot in the leg by one of Terell's crew. Lil J and his crew now wanted revenge on Terell for what they believed to be a setup. Everyone in East Oakland was looking for Terell and he knew it.

When the opportunity came for Terell to get away to Camp Akili, he jumped at it. While he did not know exactly what to expect at camp, he knew that staying at home could cost him his life. In many ways, young people don't know what to expect when they first arrive at camp. The brief farewell from a parent or guardian and the nearly 2-hour bus ride is usually not enough to prepare young people for what they will experience over the 5 days. This is probably why when they finally arrive they put on the hoods from their sweatshirts and greet the energetic counselors with a groggy "wuz up." Terell commented:

> I remember my first time coming to camp, I didn't want to participate in any of the workshops. I remember some of the counselors kept walking up to me asking me what was wrong. They would sit down and talk to me, but I was not feeling this camp. I wasn't used to that type of environment because in the streets blacks don't trust each other like that. So I had the same mentality when I came to camp, I didn't trust anyone there! On top of that, there were people trying to kill me, which is why I came to camp in the first place. I was very nervous about the whole thing.

Not only did Terell not trust people at the camp, he felt that he had been tricked by his sister, who had explained to him that he would be going to a wilderness camp to get away. Being that he loved the outdoors, Terell agreed to come. After the 1st day he quickly realized that the camp was not at all about wildlife but more about social issues.

> My sister tricked me, and told me that I was going fishing and all this stuff, you know, a real camp, like hiking and going into the woods and stuff. She heard about camp on the radio and heard

other folks talking about it so she thought it would be good for me. So I'm thinking I'm about to go have fun, like I was getting ready to go, like when I first got to camp I was like this ain't what I thought it would be, my sister tricked me! I was ready to go home. The first 2 days I was ready to go home, but the 3rd day the information started to sink in a little bit.

For many youth who come to Camp Akili, their first reaction is to distrust and resist everything they are asked to do. Unlike the draconian rules at their schools the camp's rules are quite simple: no weapons, no drugs, no smoking, no boys in girls' dorms and vice versa. In 15 years, the camp has sent home fewer than 10 youth for violating of these rules. As Terell mentioned, he couldn't trust anyone, because he was used to keeping his guard up while in the streets, so the games, icebreakers and discussions took some time to get used to. On the 2nd day, Terell came to understand the type of community that was being created at camp, which drew his interest toward the information offered during the workshops.

I realized what they were saying was the truth. This was all new to me but it made sense. I was so used to hearing negative instead of positive stuff about black people. I wasn't used to seeing a whole bunch of black people that loved and cared for each other. I'm used to black people not liking, not trusting, each other, so that was all new to me, a whole new experience, so I had to get used to opening up to people.

Many of the workshops and discussion groups at the camp are designed to provide political education about forms of structural inequality. The sessions sometimes begin with a hip-hop video or a song to illustrate the topic being discussed. The topic of racial oppression, for example, does not simply explore white oppression of blacks, but also how black youth oppress themselves. Such topics lead to a form of truth telling; raw honesty builds a culture in the community and awakens young people to the complexity of how oppression gets played out in their lives. Thomson suggests that telling the truth about oppression, rather than protecting young people from it, has been a moral ethic central to black communal life. "To prepare Black children to know themselves as Black, as part of a strong community, and as specifically *not* what a racist world would have them believe, their caregivers must start from the kind of powerful knowledge and mother-wit associated with communal elders" (1995, p. 29). Terell stated:

I remember Macheo [one of the adult counselors] told me that basically they just took us up out of your environment so you can see what life is supposed to be about. He told me that they took us away so that they could tell us that we've been lied to by society, by what we see on the streets. It's not the truth. He was givin' it to me straight.

Honest truth-telling and authentic discussions about real-life experiences with oppression form among participants a sense of respect in the community. Young people feel, If you respect me enough to tell me the truth, then I have greater respect for you. Thomson warns us that avoiding difficult discussions and conflict in the name of niceness forfeits the possibility of authentic communion, and that black youth may regard the avoidance of racism and oppression as a betrayal of trust. Terell noted:

Camp Akili makes you think about a lot of things, I can't describe it. It's like it's something that you can't describe, one of those heartfelt things that you have no words for. They tell you the truth about stuff. Like with your job or at school, they keep a lot of information from you. You know, they don't give you the real history in the book. They might as well burn that because half the stuff in there doesn't really tell you what you need to know.

This form of truth telling has been a vital aspect of African American ethic and survival. Ward claims that black communities and families have learned to "skillfully weave lessons of critical consciousness into moments of intimacy between parent and child and to cultivate resistance against beliefs, attitudes, and practices that can erode a positive identity development" (2000, pp. 50–51). In black communities, intimate conversations while braiding hair or shopping for clothes, or just eating a meal are political spaces because they create openings in which to teach black youth what it means to be black in white America. Similarly, Camp Akili re-creates these intimate conversations through structured activities and dialogue about issues in their lives.

While political education and truth telling are important ingredients in building community, the counselors at the camp also play a significant role in this effort. The young adult counselors are carefully recruited to reflect the culture of the camp participants. Social class, education level, sexuality, neighborhood, and history of incarceration are all important variables necessary to authentically connect with youth. Some counselors are college students, while others are on probation. Some are community

activists, others social service workers. In order to create meaningful connections, youth need to be able to see counselors with whom they can identify. Dereca, the executive director, commented on the camp's counselors:

> A large number of the adults come from the same communities as
> the youth. This is a critical piece of the process. So when young
> people see someone just a little bit older than them, from the same
> kind of environment that they are from, wearing the same kind of
> clothes, speaking the [same] language, and [listening to] the same
> kind of music, all that cultural stuff allows for them to feel a little
> bit more comfortable to express themselves and open up.

These counselors make it possible to create the space to share painful
experiences and be supported by a loving community. However, it is not
simply their role at the camp that makes this possible, but also how they
engage, interact, and work with the young people. The interaction between
young people and adults is influenced by Freirian pedagogy, which encourages action and reflection and avoids what Freire has called the "bank-
ing model" of education, whereby the educator deposits knowledge into
empty vessels. Rather, counselors are trained to not present themselves as
if they had all the answers, but to be real, and struggle with issues with the
youth. This means that counselors will cry, become angry, and share painful experiences as well. These authentic conversations reveal to young
people that the issues that they are discussing are real and create the safety
for them to share as well. The idea of decentering power from adults is one
way to begin to heal what has been called the generation gap. Dereca provides a timely explanation of this approach:

> When youth and adults share an experience that exposes their raw
> emotions together this begins to mend the generation gap. The
> generation gap is about the adults lecturing to the young people
> and telling them about how great it was in the good old days.
> Adults are always telling youth how messed up their society is and
> how the youth today messed it up. Adults always want youth to
> change and rarely look at fixing themselves. Very rarely do adults
> say that it was very messed up for me as a child too. Or that they
> feel a lot of pain about what's going on right now. Like I'm sad
> about Katrina or I'm mad about the direction that hip-hop is in.
> Adults talk about youth as the future and themselves as the past,
> but nobody is living in the present. So these experiential workshops
> give adults and young people the chance to be in the present with
> each other. And that's kind of what's missing from the hip-hop

generation gap. So when one of our young adult counselors stands up at the violence workshop and talks about holding one of his best friends in his arms until he died, that creates a whole opening in the room for others to share their similar experiences. When another adult counselor talks about seeing his little baby stepbrother stabbed to death and cries, this is a young man in his 20s who cries profusely and is comforted by someone like me, then the young men at the camp feel like it's okay for them to cry. They feel like, Somebody here has got my back. I think another part of having that relationship at Camp Akili is about having a sense of a bigger community that could hold all of this pain and emotion because there are 100 of us at camp with 100 black folks. A lot of the young people have never been in a space with 100 black folks so that's a healing space. Having 100 black folks in a room doing something positive or even talking about being black is something that these young people have never experienced. So that container is what makes what we do possible.

Camp Akili creates a space where being black, young, and poor are not liabilities; rather, these identities are fertile soil for the seeds of activism and social justice. The space is created by truth telling and honesty that form bonds of mutual respect between youth and adults. These dynamics are made possible because adults are willing to enter into the community not as "wise elders" but rather as "guides" who create the conversations, safety, and trust for youth to openly share their pain, hopes, and dreams. By adults' revealing their own pain around trauma, youth connect to each other and to adults in meaningful ways.

THE POWER OF RITUAL: CREATING COMMUNITY THROUGH COLLECTIVE EXPERIENCE

It is 8:00 a.m. on the 3rd day of camp and I am exhausted from 2 days of nonstop workshops and informal rap sessions. The sun is bright, and nearly 100 people from the entire camp are standing is a large circle in a meadow surrounded by gigantic redwood trees. The fragrance of pine, the sun on my face, and the cool morning air makes me smile for a second. Suddenly one of the counselors yells out the morning's chant, "Who you riding for? The red, black, and green! I love my people, yeah." In unison, all 100 of us shout back the phrase "We riding for the red, black, and green! We love our people, yeahhh!" We all clap and continue the chant with jubilance, without restraint, and everyone is smiling and laughing.

Somé reminds us that "ritual is a tribute to the human capacity to create, remember, and imagine, and to apply that imagination to the benefit
of community" (1999, p. 36). I use the term "ritual" to convey the notion
that carefully choreographed experiences such as experiential activities or
workshops, discussions, or visualizations can serve as powerful gateways
to self, social, and spiritual awareness. These rituals form the basis of the
camp and are used to foster communal healing. They are carefully designed activities, workshops, and profound experiences that awaken
young people's political consciousness, build ethnic identity, and form
healthy relationships.

Often these rituals serve to unite community because they provide a
common experience for all community members. Similar to a natural di-
saster, a death, or a tragedy such as September 11th, these events bring
people together in profound ways because our fragile exteriors are stripped
away to reveal our raw humanity. The rituals at Camp Akili were created
to simulate the intensity of such an event in order to foster collective consciousness about a particular issue. Somé notes, "Ritual is by its nature a
communal activity and an act of creation. . . . The ritual must create a certain kind of energy that can embrace the individuals involved, allowing
them to expand their awareness and undergo the transformation necessary to become healed" (1999, p. 35). The raw emotion, honest dialogue,
and sharing forms bonds and adds meaning to being in community because
individuals surrender and shed their cloaks, created by trauma. The young
people's sharing gives permission for others to testify, which build trust
in the community. This collective trust allows individuals to feel that they
can share to the community without being judged. Their sharing is both
an opportunity to heal and a moment of choice to reclaim and resurrect
ways of being in the world.

Camp Akili employed numerous rituals throughout the 5 days, from
simple icebreakers to the more dramatic collective reenactment of the Middle
Passage, of the African slave trade. These rituals create an opportunity for
young people to rediscover their collective identities and foster new forms
of political consciousness. The experiential activities force, encourage, and
foster intensely personal reflection and introspection among youth about
internalized social trauma. Dereca described the context of how these rituals
function at Camp Akili:

> One really obvious thing is that we listen. I think that most work-
> shops, the lectures, are designed to talk to youth and they tell youth
> what to think, what they feel, why they feel that way. There is no
> part where the participant gets to share, and really *share* their
> feelings and thoughts. I think our rituals and experiential work-

shops are designed so that the participant shares. It's about the participants in the room and finding that commonality through collective sharing. What makes this process so powerful is that we are tapping into collective pain and collectively sharing our experiences of that pain and providing some space for that. Which alone is healing. Just being there and holding each other and giving each other tissues, but it really is that cathartic collective sharing of pain. Any group that goes through that, whether it's survivors of a plane crash or an earthquake, you have to sit there and share this with the next guy; that's painful and it bonds to you.

These rituals and activities encourage another important ingredient at camp, which is the space to testify, to give voice to pain, and be supported in the process by other community members. Dereca discussed the impact of these rituals:

It's hard to dismiss people who are crying because three of their brothers had got shot. When you talk about violence, in that personal way, it's so raw that it makes you want to turn away. It's like too much to deal with, too much to handle and it feels like you are forever changed by hearing people's personal stories and that's why the relationships are so strong.

One of these activities is a visualization and experiential reenactment of the part of the Atlantic slave trade called the Middle Passage. The idea behind this ritual was for black youth to understand the impact of the slave trade and to discuss the legacy of this historical event in their daily lives. The activity encouraged black youth to rethink, for example, why they use the term "nigga" and where the term originated. The reenactment provided them with the experience of how it must have felt to be bought and sold or to have their children taken away.

The Middle Passage Ritual

In a 3,000-square-foot auditorium all the lights were turned off as participants were guided through a visualization of what it might have been like living in Africa 400 years ago. Through taped music, orchestrated sound effects, carefully arranged fragrances such as incense, and selected physical objects such as chains and ropes, youth were guided through a vivid reenactment of the Middle Passage. The activity re-created the removal of Africans from the continent of Africa and the 3- to 4-month voyage as human cargo in the dank, filthy bowels of European slave ships. In a large room with a bare floor, all the youth were blindfolded and led through a narrated visualization accompanied by music and other sounds. The visualization began with a narration of being in Africa, with peaceful music, and of being connected to family, villages, and community. Everyone held hands and listened to the peaceful narration of living in a village and learning from elders. The music dramatically changed, marking the end of tranquility. Youth who had been holding hands were suddenly pulled apart and pushed around, still blindfolded, the sound of chains rattling in the background. Then they were forced to the ground, body to body, accompanied by the sound of screaming and moaning, simulating being captured and loaded onto slave ships. The visualization intensified with traveling to the auction block and on to plantations, with the sounds of whips and reminders of terrible loss and grief. The visualization continued with contemporary urban trauma and the sound of gunshots and of hearing terms like "my nigga" and "what up nigga?" which represent the present-day internalization of racism.

The visualization ended with a large circle, everyone holding hands again to the backdrop of uplifting music. With the lights still off, candles were placed in front of all 100 participants and when the blindfolds were removed, they saw the light from the candles placed in front of them. Afterward, some young people cried quietly, others were silent, but all were deeply moved by the experience. They discussed what the activity felt like and what they learned from the experience. Malik, one of the 16-year-old participants from Oakland, commented on his experience of the activity:

> Before I came here, I didn't know what the term "nigga" meant, and I didn't really care. I would say, "What's up, nigga," "What you doin,' nigga?" I had no idea of what the term meant or where it came from. I didn't know how our ancestors felt when the white man called us "nigger." I thought about it differently after this activity. To be tied up and pulled around in the dark, it made me understand how it must have felt to be treated like we were dogs, like we were animals. It hurts to know that our people have experienced this. But you don't realize this until you experience something like this activity, even for just an hour. I learned that we call each other that word without knowing the price black folks paid.

Malik's awareness of the historical legacy of the term "nigga" sparked an understanding of racial unity while at the same time politicized his understanding of black youth oppression. Activities such as these encourage youth to make connections to historical racial oppression and present-day racial issues. Some youth made explicit connections between the violence experienced by Africans through slavery and present-day violence in urban communities. This collective racial identity provided youth with a broader political conscious-ness about social issues. Additionally, it fostered a greater sense of collective responsibility and purpose and the desire to create a higher quality of life for themselves and their communities. Similarly, Jasmon reflected on her experi-ence with the Middle Passage ritual:

> That was crazy, I never when through something which made me feel like it really happened! The activity made me feel like we [Africans] were treated like dogs, like we were animals. You can't really experience that anywhere. Even though it wasn't actually happening to us, I just felt for a short amount of time how it must have felt for Africans. I know what it feels like to be separated from everybody you know. How it felt to actually be tied up and pulled around. Our ancestors had to go through being slaves, being called "nigger" and now we calling ourselves that! It makes me wish I could do something. It never really hit me until I went through something like that activity.

Sometimes it takes a while for youth to process, reflect on, and think about the meaning of the Middle Passage ritual. Often, during this reflec-tion, youth develop a historical consciousness about racial oppression and its legacy. There is an incredible intelligence created in emotional energy. Whether they are confused, angry, sad, or bewildered, the activity forces youth to think in new ways about their identities, question the use of the term "nigga," and understand the social and spiritual impact of the slave trade on black people throughout the world. This political consciousness is an important starting point for young people to change their behavior. Jasmon commented:

> You don't learn that until you experience something like camp. I would say "nigga" because I didn't know any better. You don't know what's right or wrong, unless you're taught that way. We're not taught about where that term comes from. So I don't say "nigga" and I learned what the word means. I taught my friends because they didn't know where the word came from. I told them about that experience, and that we are hurting our ancestors when we say "nigga."

Rituals like that of the Middle Passage provide opportunities for youth to make connections between such historical events as the slave trade and present-day issues. For Jasmon, not using the term "nigga" constituted a new way to demonstrate respect to other black youth and for herself. She viewed this form of respect as vital for survival and success.

Other rituals focus entirely on contemporary day-to-day life issues. For example, we believed that sexual abuse, sexism and misogyny together constituted a major barrier to the collective healing process. We believed that if youth and young adults could confront the tensions, anxiety, and contradictions of gender politics, the community could take a significant step toward collective consciousness about oppression. This ritual involved another powerful experience designed to jolt young people's consciousness about the ways in which sexism is reproduced in black youth culture.

I Am My Sister's Keeper: The Sexism Ritual

The sexism ritual begins with discussions about sexism, gender, and misogyny in a classroom setting. The group views videos, advertisements, commercials, and magazine photos of black women and discusses the images as they examine terms that are used to describe women. The ritual was designed to expose young men's attitudes about sexism and shift the gendered power dynamics so that young women could openly share their firsthand, often painful, experiences with sexism. The ritual requires that young men and women separated into their own groups to have different conversations about the pain, rage, anger, and frustration that comes from sexism. In circles, women share both horrifying stories of rape and molestation and dreams of how they want to be treated by men. The men discuss the challenges of how their distorted views about manhood are often defined by the mistreatment of women. The ritual culminates with the "gender walk," which is a gauntlet where the young women form two lines. The young women are instructed to shout anything that has been said to them by a male to each young man as he passes between them. Without knowing what the young women have been instructed to do, each male at the camp is instructed to walk alone through the gauntlet. The young women shout out phrases such as "You got a nice ass!" "Bitches ain't shit" or "I never told you I loved you!"

At first, each young man laughs as he walks through until he hears something that pierces his fragile exterior. One young woman shouts to each young man as he passed, with fury in her voice, "Hurry up, man, it's my turn," repeating what one of her assailants had said when she had been raped. Another shouts, "If you shut up it won't hurt" reiterating a comment from her own sexual abuse. It's not simply hearing the phrases from these young women that makes this ritual so powerful; it's also feeling the frustration, hurt, and pain behind each word. As the young men walk down this line and hear the things that women were told by other men every day, they are shocked into consciousness about the issues that women are forced to deal with on a daily basis.

While the experience might be different for everyone, afterward, everyone is changed. The young men all describe the same experience of feeling like a piece of meat or feeling a sense of powerlessness for just those few minutes. The young women explain the feeling of being empowered to testify to what they feel and hear every day.

After the walk through both groups are brought back together in a large room to discuss the experience. The young men are seated on the floor and surrounded by a large circle of chairs where the young women are seated. The young men, feeling frustrated and angry, are told that they must simply listen without responding to what the women say to them. This process forces young men to listen to what young women are saying and to experience the real rawness of young women's frustration and pain. The young women testify about their experiences with sexism and share their stories with the community in brutal honesty. This unveils the trauma that they have experienced as a community and it is raw and naked for everyone to see. Janasha, a 17-year-old camp participant, stated:

> When we are out on these streets we have to deal with this shit all by ourselves, and nobody protects us. We might even call ourselves bitches, but it all has to stop. I want to say to the brothers here that are crying with us, I know you feel it, and I respect that because at least you are man enough to show that you feel what we go through.

Rituals such as these open space for youth to confront traumatic experiences and creates an environment for open discussion, dialogue, and support for one another as they process what they collectively experienced. The circle provides a vehicle for youth to release the pain they have held while at the same time they are supported by each other. Another young woman commented about the silent young men seated in front of her.

> I just hope you felt some of our pain, and some of our love too, because we [women] have to teach y'all. We are here for y'all [men] and we want you to be here for us as well because we need you.

Terell learned something new about himself after this ritual. His alert body language and the intensity in his eyes conveyed that something powerful was happening to him. He talked about his experience of the ritual:

> Afterward I didn't have the same mind frame. I have called many girls "bitches," "hoes," right in they face, but didn't know it made

them feel like that. I felt bad because all the girls were crying and upset at how we men have treated them. It really made me think; it was deep because we had to sit there and think and face all everyone who had been hurt. It's given me a lot to think about.

These rituals encourage intensely personal reflection and introspection about internalized social trauma because they pierce through the thin veil of hardness and shatter the "tough fronts" used for surviving urban life. The learning and discussions after this ritual are not gender specific. Both the young men and the young women take with them important lessons. Testifying and baring witness to collective pain releases a profound and extraordinary energy in an environment that allows young people to be free to share and be freed in doing so. Terell reflected on his camp experience:

Camp to me is basically like, "get-right" camp. It shows us the mirror image of where we are today, and where we need to be in the future. The sexism workshop showed us where we are as a people. I think that's the mirror of who we are. Looking in the mirror and where we need to be, for example, was revealed to us when the sisters started crying and stuff and showed us how we as men inflict pain on them and we may not even be conscious of that! That's where we need to be. We need to be conscious of that kind of stuff. It was a healthy experience. It's almost like, the movie *Sankofa* where the lady ran into the little chamber and learned about her history by showing what her ancestors had been through. When she came out of the chamber she was conscious of who she was.

NO SET TRIPPIN'! THE POWER OF COMMUNITY

For Terell, his escape from Oakland was also his rescue. Had other people not been looking for revenge, he might never have attended Camp Akili. However, doing so allowed him to see a different type of community life for himself and his crew. The camp created an environment where youth from different turfs—West Oakland, East Oakland—gang affiliations, and high schools created one unified community of trust, love, and respect. Terell declared:

I see things different now. You know, no set trippin'! I have friends from different places. I think that's real important because a lot of times we are broken up by neighborhood, high school, city, or even district: East Oakland, West Oakland, North Oakland. We get broken up by so many divisions. By the end of camp, people feel like a family, almost like we are relatives, you know. I think that that's real important because I never really felt anything like that before. I think it's important for people to feel like that. Even if I never came to camp ever again, it showed me that something like that can be built in a short amount of time if we really put our hearts and work into it. And that was only 5 days. Just think if we stayed together 5 weeks how powerful that would have been! Five months, 5 years, you know. I mean, it just showed me that anything is possible!

Terell had developed numerous friendships at the camp and saw himself as a member of a new community. His new community was different from that of his friends who had shot Lil J. While he loved his crew, he also knew that unless they shared his new values, identity, and way of seeing the world, he would soon part ways with them. His new friends and community gave Terell a support system where he could have new conversations, participate in positive activities, and take on real problems in his community. Some of his crosstown rivals were at the camp, and he connected with them in ways that would have never happened on the streets:

When you go through certain things with people it breaks down some boundaries. Just the fact that people going through different experiences knowing that they are not alone helps a lot. To some extent we latched onto each other, you know, and I think that's how it happened. That's how it happened in my group, you know. The 1st day, we didn't have anything to really talk about. Once we started going through different activities, we were able to relate to each other and we had something real to talk about. That's when we started opening up and let all our boundaries down.

Opening up wasn't something Terell was used to doing. In fact, he commented that "where I come from it's not okay to cry; it can get you killed." Several youth in his group at camp agreed with him. To prove it, one young man shared a story about being brought into a crack house by his mother when he was 8 years old. He described the darkness of the house where people were smoking and he watched his mom get high until she passed out. "There was a guy in the house that was bothering me and he took out a syringe and he threatened to stick me with it." His mother had given him a gun, in case something happened while she was smoking. Being 8 years old and frightened, he held the gun up to protect himself and shot and killed the man who was threatening him. He said, "My mom was so high that she didn't even know what happened." He left the crack house with his mother and never cried about it until he shared the traumatic incident at Camp Akili. "I cried for hours," he related, "and I guess all that was bottled up in me." Terell identified how stories like these and supporting each other allowed him and other youth to "let the walls down" and connect with each other in ways they didn't know was possible:

> It's almost like a consciousness training ground, almost like a boot camp. Not in a military sense, but like a boot camp in the sense that you come from the community and you come from all these messed-up type of conditions. You come to this camp where you leave that situation to be able to look back at it and then see if you want to change it or how you wanna change it.

There is a dilemma in creating these types of experiences for black youth. On the one hand, creating a beloved community provides an opportunity for youth to see themselves, their original community, and society in new ways. On the other hand, the conditions of their communities are the same, and when they return, they are thrust back into the throes of reality. Terell recalled his dramatic return from camp:

> I remember when I got home, I really just started shedding tears as soon as I walked through the door because I was back here in my neighborhood. I didn't want to go back home. I wanted to stay in that beautiful environment with the trees and the water and the black people loving each other. Like the 1st day of camp, nobody trusted each other. But on the last day we were all brothers and sisters. Playing, laughing, joking with each other. You know what I'm saying? I didn't want to leave that. That was so beautiful to me. It was my first time really seeing something like that in my life. Leaving that environment kind of hurt me because I had to go back to my world, to the real world. The reality out here on the streets is that black people don't trust each other, but camp just showed us the truth, and how it's supposed to be. After you know how its supposed to be, and then to go back to the way that it is, it hurts.

Struggling to make sense of his return back to Oakland, Terell said:

> All I cared about was surviving and getting some money. But what Camp Akili did was it took me away from that to a beautiful-ass place. I remember the way that I felt, that feeling is still with me. That feeling is like my hope, it lets me know that there's hope out here, because I felt it!

Terell was able to stay with his cousin in Sacramento for a few weeks until Lil J's crew had stopped looking for him. When he returned, he immediately came to the Leadership Excellence office and started attending one of the support groups. During one of the sessions he noted:

> I want to take the initiative and start talking to younger youth about this stuff. I want to use my critical thinking and start going to school again. I'm working on myself and my attitude and I've come a long way, and I have my head on straight. I can be a walking example of it. So I have to walk the walk and talk the talk to help these young brothers and sisters out now.

For the time being, Terell's life had got back on track. While he had to navigate between his crew in East Oakland and his new community in Leadership Excellence, he had developed a passion to get more involved with community issues. His new relationships served as pathways to new possibilities for his life.

HEALING AND NEW TEXTURES OF SOCIAL CAPITAL

Perhaps there is something about healthy, vibrant, strong communities that fosters hope, imagination, and new ways of seeing the world. For Terell, and hundreds of other youth who have participated in Camp Akili, the camp experience recalibrates what is possible for their own lives and their communities. The community at Camp Akili is less about simply bringing black youth together than about creating a collective consciousness about racial identity, sexism, violence, and activism. "If we can build something like this in 5 days, imagine what we could do in 5 weeks, or 5 months." Terell's comment accurately captures the spirit of possibility and energy for social change that young people often describe after camp.

The trauma black youth experience can be healed by their collectively sharing their trauma and through providing youth with the political education to "contextualize" the pain they experience. This process contributes to a more radical notion of community and political consciousness. After camp, young people participate in a number of other Leadership Excellence programs that further develop their political consciousness. Through weekly support groups or academic support programs at their local school, the organization seeks to funnel their energy into youth organizing efforts or other community projects.

Counselors lead youth at Camp Akili with chants during a community building activity. All photos © Bryan Farley.

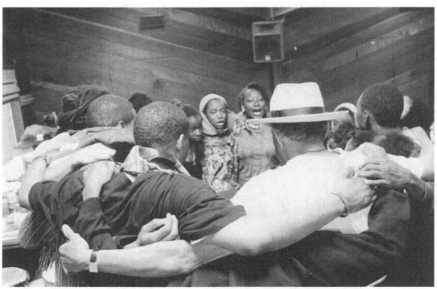

Youth from Oakland bond at Camp Akili after sharing their personal stories.

Leadership Excellence students pose in front of the Kwame Nkrumah memorial in Accra, Ghana

Leadership Excellence counselor embraces a young man after discussion about manhood.

Leadership Excellence staffers take a break to pose for a picture outside the office in downtown Oakland.

Youth from Leadership Excellence march to protest the shooting of an unarmed black youth in Oakland.

Youth from Camp Akili prepare to return home to Oakland.

Young woman singing
during a community
building activity at
Camp Akili.

4

Creating Consciousness Through Black Masculinity

How does it feel to be a problem?

W.E.B. Du Bois, *The Souls of Black Folk*

Vince told me today that for years he hated his father for leaving him and his mother. But last week Vince had finally developed enough nerve to go up to the county jail and confront his father, whom he had not seen in more than 10 years. He told me that the emotional confrontation ended up with both of them crying and embracing each other. He hoped that this reconciliation would begin to develop the relationship he had longed for.

—Field notes, August 2004

AS WE WERE DRIVING from the grocery store to our home in East Oakland, my 7-year-old daughter noticed a group of African American teens hanging out on a corner near our neighborhood. The cool fall weather had settled into the Bay Area so all the young men were wearing large gray or black jackets with hoods. As we turned the corner and passed by the group of young men, my daughter asked, "Daddy, are they dangerous?" I retrained myself from being shocked at her question and pretended that I didn't know whom she was talking about. I replied, "Are who dangerous, honey?" As she wiped the ice cream from her face, she pointed toward the group of five young men and said, "Those men right there, are they dangerous?" I replied, "Why do you think they are dangerous, honey? They don't seem to be bothering anyone." Her question deeply concerned me. How could my own daughter simply look at a group of black youth and conclude that they might be dangerous? How could I have contributed to her stereotype about black youth in Oakland? She knew numerous black youth from my work in the community and from attending Saturday morning activities at Leadership Excellence. I asked her to explain to me why she thought the group of young men might be dangerous. She replied, "Because I always see the police always take them away." I realized that despite her personal connections and her relationships with black youth through my work, her perceptions of black youth were influenced by television, observations of police interactions, and our family conversations about several young people who had burglarized some homes in our neighborhood. The fact of the matter was that there was very little in her environment to offer a more positive image of black youth in Oakland.

Unfortunately, the notion that black youth are a menace to society is fostered in the public consciousness and reinforced through public policy. Nightly news stories of shootings involving young black men, films that depict black youth as dangerous criminals, and newspaper reports of rising crime among black teens all contribute to the negative image of black youth. These images are reinforced by racist fears of black people and have a powerful impact on public policy. For example, although blacks constitute only 7.3% of San Francisco's population, they made up more than 50% of the total arrests in 2005, the highest in California.[1] Experts suggest that this trend is the result of policing practices that target black neighborhoods and misperceptions about black youth and crime. Male Males (1999) suggests that despite declining youth crime, public policy continues to invest in controlling and containing youth.

Reinforcing the concept of a black youth menace, celebrities such as Oprah Winfrey and Bill Cosby have criticized black youth for not valuing education (Powell, 2007). While Oprah's extraordinary philanthropic efforts should be applauded, her comments about black youth in inner-city America valuing their sneakers more than education raise serious concerns about her views of black youth. Oprah's comments do not consider three important ideas regarding black youth. First, the lack of investment in their lives has resulted in dismal social, health, and educational outcomes. Second, black youth do not all have the same experiences; with the ample support, opportunities, and vision, black youth can excel socially and academically. Third, when young people are involved in solving problems in their communities, they develop stronger identities and healthier communities in the process.

There is no doubt that African American males face a number of obstacles to educational success, economic mobility, and well-being (Littles, Bowers, & Gilmer, 2008; Noguera, 2008; Young, 2004). Structural barriers such as poor-quality schools and fewer job opportunities have made the life chances for black males more difficult than those of their white counterparts. These structural barriers are sometimes reinforced by negative perceptions held by employers, police, and teachers (Wilson, 1996b). Often, these perceptions of young black men are based in fear that they are dangerous, a threat to public safety. Copious research has shown how sentencing laws, policing practices, and public policy have all contributed to disproportionate numbers of adjudicated black men (Brunson & Miller, 2006; Mincy, 2006; Young, 2004). Scholars have illustrated how film, television news, and even social science research has portrayed young black males in ways that reinforce negative perceptions (Hutchinson, 1994). Images of young black men have "a way of maintaining themselves in the public's mind and in the absence of quality information and analyses, these images have become the primary prisms through which people construct an understanding of social reality" (Sánchez-Jankowski, 1991, p. 288).

In particular, social science research has contributed to negative perceptions as researchers have become entirely focused on describing and predicting behavior such as violence, aggression, idleness, and survival strategies. This myopic negative focus on young black men has a long tradition in social science research. Structural transformations in the economy, migration from the South to the North, and urban problems have all prompted researchers to understand both the challenges and opportunities that shape black men's lives. Du Bois's "The Study of the Negro Problem" (1898) and, later, *The Philadelphia Negro* (1899), provided two of the earliest, theoretically informed ethnographies of black urban life. Early in his career, Du Bois was interested in describing the conditions and behaviors within black communities that he believed contributed to urban problems. For Du Bois, black social problems could be explained largely as a result of the impact of enslavement and its reverberating effects on black progress and the social environment could be explained through the nuances found in customs, behaviors, physical surroundings, and work patterns. He wrote:

> We have two great causes for the present conditions of the Negro: Slavery and emancipation with their attendant phenomena of ignorance, lack of discipline and moral weakness . . . [and] the physical surrounding of house and home and ward, the moral encouragements and discouragements which he encounters. (p. 283)

Du Bois's conclusions about problems in black life involve two fundamental elements that continue to shape the intellectual groundwork for the study of black communities in general, and black men in particular. First, black problems can be best conceptualized as a "symptom" of broader social, economic, and *structural* factors. Thus, crime, violence, and moral decay are not endemic to black communities, but rather result from *structural disruption*, a term that describes how institutions, systems, and the economy disrupt patterns of daily life. Second, the environment and social settings in which black men go about their daily lives are rich with *cultural* information that can help us to better understand behaviors, attitudes, and beliefs in black communities.

More recently, the tensions between *cultural* explanations of black life, which focus on values, beliefs, and attitudes, and *structural* explanations, that is, of how economic shifts and the scarcity of work shape behavior, have largely been reformulated in ways that focus more attention on the structural factors as primary explanation of sustained poverty. Still research continues to frame young black males as contentious and to define their behavior through tough postures, potential violence, and maladaptive behaviors. These images fail to capture the mosaic of experiences and textured realities of young black men's lives. The focus has resulted in an "exceptionally myopic view of [black men's] humanity" (Young, 2004, p. 20). Unfortunately, these discussions about black men's lives are restricted to static conceptualizations of masculinity, rigid frames about work and family life, and distorted views about behavior.

The persistent intellectual and public fetish of the problems of young black males has grossly obscured an understanding of social and behavioral assets shared among young black men regardless of social class and income. Vince's brave emotional reconciliation with his father illustrates another lens by which to understand black men's relationships with one another. Vince's story raises questions regarding alternative ways in which young black men care for one another, share advice, and develop their beliefs about manhood. Emerging research has recently given us a rare glimpse into the worldviews and meaning making about black men's lives and aspirations (Young, 2004). This research illustrates how individuals can act upon their environment (Smith, 2007; Young, 2004) and navigates between structural and cultural explanations of behavior. By focusing on agency, the capacity to make choices and act, this perspective demonstrates how black men make meaning out of dire situations and sometimes act to change their life chances.

Young's work is important because it extends our perspective about young black male behavior beyond the conceptual boundaries of labor, crime, and notions of extinction. This perspective captures alternative ways in which young black men go about their daily lives in ways that challenge our stereotypes of black masculinity. Critical consciousness is the capacity to think about the root causes of social problems and act to create equality and justice for the common good. For African American males, critical consciousness can deconstruct oppressive beliefs about black manhood and build healthy, and just, views of gender.

This chapter explores the ways in which young black men (aged 15–20) in an all-male after-school support group discuss their fathers, manhood, racism, violence, and rage with love, compassion, and care. Building from Athena Mutua's (2006) notion of progressive black masculinities, I illustrate how the support group after Camp Akili builds upon the political and cultural self-awareness created at camp to change beliefs about manhood and masculinity. This chapter illustrates how the convergence of the personal and political dimensions of black masculinity among African American young males fosters new forms of political activism.

STORIES OF OUR FATHERS

I was somewhat surprised that there were only 12 young men at the Men Educating and Creating Action (MECA) support group tonight when I arrived. Bilal, the program coordinator, had told me several times about the powerful and insightful discussion the youth would have during the Thursday night meetings. There were no predefined topics during the MECA support group. Young men would show up and the facilitator would begin to check in with everyone. Someone's comment would spark a conversation that would lead to a larger group discussion. Sometimes they would talk about a new movie, other times they would talk about girls. MECA was a place where the young men could be themselves and talk about whatever was on their mind.

The discussions were usually facilitated by Bilal, a streetwise, self-educated 30-year-old man who worked part time for Leadership Excellence and part time for Federal Express at the Oakland Airport. His ability to navigate the streets earned him a great deal of respect among the young men at MECA. During the support group sessions, Bilal would challenge the young men's preconceived notions of manhood. His constant questioning and prodding would force the young men to think deeply about static ideas about manhood.

One night, the conversation focused on the young men's fathers. Some of the young men held animosity toward their fathers, while others commented about how fortunate they were to have their fathers in their lives. I was particularly struck by the level of insight, wisdom, and reflection that came from two of the young men during these meetings. Marcus and Vince have been best friends since the fifth grade. Marcus is heavyset and looks much older than his 18 years. He says that he uses his mature look to talk to much older women. Vince is much shorter than Marcus and has a sense of humor that always catches me by surprise. The first night I attended the MECA program, I decided to wear a shirt that I had purchased in Brazil. The unfinished cotton and the zigzag string that closes the V-neck, gave the shirt a rather old-world look. When Vince saw me he immediately commented, "Man, you look like you just stepped out of a Lord of the Rings movie! Nobody wears shirts like that!" To this day, I refuse to wear that shirt.

Marcus and Vince discussed their relationships with their fathers. Vince commented:

> Well, my dad has been a criminal since he was a young boy. He used to tell me when he was in elementary school, he shot a kid and has been in and out of jail ever since. When I was growing up, he was in and out of jail all the time, so I really didn't know him. I don't really have a relationship with my father because I don't think he cares. He doesn't even call us, or when he comes to Oakland to go to my grandmother's house he doesn't call us to tell us that he's out here. Birthdays we don't see him, Christmas we don't see him, New Year's we don't see him.

Some of the young men in the group identified with Vince's story because they also had poor relationships with their fathers. The young men shared similar stories but Bilal pushed them further and asked them what they missed by not having their fathers around. A few of the young men resisted at first and commented that they didn't miss anything, because their fathers couldn't teach them anything about life. A few, however, thought about Bilal's question. After reflecting, Vince said:

> I want my father to just be there, to have him to just listen and help. I wouldn't really want him to baby me, or to do everything that everybody else's father does. I just want to see him from time to time, and I just want him to help my mom. I just want him to help out and be there. I'm older now and I can do things for myself but when I needed someone to fall on I would have liked for him to be there. For example, when I went to jail for the first time, he was just getting out of jail. My mom, three sisters, and my niece and nephew were staying in a motel and we all had to chip in and pay rent. My mom was selling dope, I was selling weed, my sister was selling dope, and everybody else was just really making money to pay rent. I got caught one night with the weed on me, so I had to go to jail. That entire time my father was not with me. I just wanted him to come to some of the court dates and tell me that it would be all right and that I could make it, but he was never there.

The feelings of abandonment and isolation that came from Vince's not having his father in his life is, unfortunately, a familiar story among some

African American youth. Vince viewed his father's capacity to "help out" and support his mother financially as an important trait of fatherhood. Part of his rationale for selling drugs was to support the family financially, a responsibility that his father had abandoned. More significant, however, was the emotional support, advice, and guidance he wanted from his father. Having his father be with him at court dates and show up on birthdays and on special occasions was another important form of support that he longed for. Vince believed that his father didn't care about him, because he had never been there for him.

Perhaps more significant than the financial support was the emotional support, guidance, and advice the young men desperately needed and deeply desired from their fathers. Often when asked about their fathers, young black men frequently respond with anger about either the relationship they wish they had with their fathers or the lack of support their fathers provided. Beneath their comments are years of disappointment, shame, fear, and hurt. Bilal asked the young men what they would say to their fathers if they were sitting in the room with them. Vince responded with anger and frustration:

> If my father were here right now, I would say to him, "Fuck you! I don't need you no more! My mom just got evicted and she probably has to go back to another motel, and you won't help us out. Once I get into college and become what I need to become, I don't want to ever hear from you and don't ask me for shit." I won't even be at your funeral!

These feelings influence how the young men see themselves as future fathers. Some commented about how hard their mothers had to work to support the family when their fathers left them. Many of the young men stated that as future fathers, they would be there to take care of their families because they knew what it was like growing up without a father around. One young man in the group related about his view of fatherhood:

> I see a father figure as a man taking the responsibility of raising his child, taking on his kids, taking care of us. My father never did that; he gave up on us. He choose drugs over us. He choose a lot of other things over us. It hurt me coming up and it made me realize that sometimes people have to make different decisions. Sometimes people are so caught up in certain scenarios that they can't help. But I just wish he would have been there for the small things like coming to my football games or showing me how to shave.

Some of the young men shared with the group the difficulties they had with their mother's attempts to discipline them. Their remarks are based in patriarchal ideas about masculinity and distorted perceptions of gender.

If my father was around, I feel like I would know my limits because he would keep me in check. But when my mom says something, I'm ready to challenge her. She is the authority figure in the house, but she is not like a male authority. I feel like she is not man enough to control me, you know? A man is supposed to have dominion, he got power, he's supposed to have control in his house. Basically, that's how I see the male role.

Many of the young men's views about gender and masculinity were influenced by patriarchal ideas of masculinity. They saw their fathers as an "ideal" masculine model who possessed power, strength, and toughness. They also spoke about a more subtle side of what they missed from not having their fathers in their lives. One young man continued discussing the difficulty he had with being raised by his mother. He spoke honestly about needing someone who understood what he was experiencing as a young man.

I wanted my dad to teach me about girls, but that never happened. I just don't feel comfortable talking to my mom about those issues because I know she can't relate. I know if my father was there, he could actually understand what I was feeling. He could guide me about things that I had to learn on my own. You can't just talk to your momma about a wet dream, come on!

Young black men being raised by their mothers or other women often look for male authority for guidance, support, and advice during their teenage years. For many young black males, they understand what they are missing from not having their fathers around. For some young men, masculinity is authority and power, while others view it as guidance and support. In some cases, uncles, older brothers, male family friends, and other male role models step in and provide the type of support needed to raise young black men. In Vince's case, however, there were few black men in his life to support him:

Frank was actually my favorite cousin and he was a role model and somebody that I looked up to. He played basketball and football throughout his high school career. He went to Merritt Community

College and he wanted to be a professional football player. He would always tell me and my little cousin to go to school. He also taught us how to play sports. But when I was 12, he got into a fatal car accident and passed away. Since then it was like I had no one to look up to. My older brother is still in jail. My cousin was gang-banging and selling dope so he wasn't really anyone to look up to. Basically that leaves me to do it myself, to find my own path.

These young men's stories about their fathers revealed their pain, disappointment, and hopes, a human side of young black men that unfortunately is rarely portrayed in the media. The stories also allowed for the young men to learn about how their peers viewed their fathers and shared similar experiences. Some of the young men in MECA did have fathers in their lives. In contrast to Vince, Marcus had a very different experience with his father, who was there for him all his life. Marcus's father was 59 when Marcus was born, so by the time Marcus reached 16, his father wasn't interested in taking him to baseball games, and he rarely disciplined him. Unlike Vince, Marcus took his father's advice, support, and guidance for granted. The MECA support group pushed Marcus to reflect on those lessons. He explained:

> My daddy was a real difficult dude to figure out while he was here. My dad died a couple of years ago. While he was here, it was really hard for me to understand the values that he was trying to teach me. He was 59 when I was born so when I was a teenager we never really went to ball games and stuff like that because he was an old dude. But I would talk to him about the news or whatever.

When Marcus's father was much younger he was known on the streets as a hustler, from running numbers. He owned a legitimate storefront TV repair shop, went to work every day, and took care of his responsibilities at home. Marcus never understood why his father was so bitter and angry at everyone. Before Marcus was born, his father had been laid off from a good-paying job at the naval shipyard in San Francisco. Two white men had lied and said that his father had been stealing expensive equipment from the shipyard. One morning when his father showed up for work, they stopped him at the gate and fired him on the spot with no evidence. From that day on, his father didn't trust white people, or anyone, for that matter.

Marcus's father died when Marcus was 17. Before his father's death, Marcus saw a range of emotions from his father. He recalled tender moments such as wrestling on the living room floor after dinner with his father, or his father teaching him how to fix a flat tire. He also recalled a time when his father fought a man for the man's saying something to his mother. On one occasion, Marcus walked into his mother and father's room, and for the first time in his life, he saw his father cry. It was shocking to Marcus because he didn't know what to say to his father, so he simply asked, "Daddy, what's wrong?" His father was sitting on the side of the bed. Before he looked up, he inhaled from the joint that he held between his fingers then explained to Marcus that James, his father's best friend, had passed. This was a significant experience for Marcus because it changed the meaning of manhood for him. Marcus explained:

> I didn't know how to react! My daddy crying? I never seen this because he was like a coldhearted kind of dude. So it hit me when I had seen my daddy cry. I realized that it was okay for me to cry. It kind of messed me up at first because I had an image of what it meant to be masculine from watching TV. I thought that a real man doesn't cry. But when I saw my dad cry, it completely changed how I thought about being a man from that point on. He was a bitter, hard-core dude but when I seen him cry, it made me see him differently, like he only human. That just stuck with me.

His father, and not the streets, shaped Marcus's view of manhood. Belying the popular depictions of black masculinity that focus on absent and emotionally distant fathers, Marcus's story demonstrates that his father played a significant role in his life and influenced his perspective of manhood. Seeing his father cry was an important turning point in his understanding of manhood because it revealed to Marcus a more human side of his father. Marcus learned a great deal from his father, but when he entered high school he began to push his father away. His father would talk to him, but Marcus didn't really care what his father was trying to teach him. His mother's work schedule and his father's age meant that by the time he was 16, he had the freedom to get involved in the streets. Marcus commented on how his father would try to lead him down the right path:

> As I got more involved with the streets my dad would tell me things that I never understood what he meant. He would say, "Boy, I could show you a fortune but I cannot make you think rich," or he always said, "You can't catch the rabbit with your dogs tied." I didn't care what he meant, I didn't want to hear it! But he just kept drilling and drilling and drilling and I just kept pushing him away so eventually it got to the point where I drifted away from him. It finally got to the point where we didn't argue anymore. I think he

honestly accepted me for what I was and he stopped preaching to me. He just let me go and let me figure life out for myself.

During the group discussion, Marcus began to cry as he remembered all the trouble he had caused his father. He explained that he never took the opportunity to tell his father he loved him, and while he knew his father loved him, they rarely shared how they felt about each other. Marcus, filled with emotion, said:

> I wish I could apologize to him because I put him through a lot of shit. I don't think that I told him how much that I really loved him. I never really got that opportunity and though I showed it, I never said it. He didn't say it, he showed it, I felt like I owed him that because there is nothing that I could do to pay him back. I could buy him a mansion but that's still not enough to show how much I loved my dad.

The stories from Marcus and Vince give us insight into how young black men think about fatherhood and masculinity. Vince's ideas about manhood came from not having a father around. For Vince, manhood primarily meant "being there" and supporting his children and family and contributing whenever possible. In contrast, Marcus had a strong, though strained, relationship with his father. He learned a great deal about fatherhood from having his father teach him life lessons.

Examining how young men's views of their fathers provides a glimpse into a social world that is rarely seen. The conversations that happen in these private spaces often break from the hard exteriors and fronts commonly used to portray black male youth. Young reminds us that "it is important to pay attention to what people articulate as their own understanding of how social processes work and how they as individuals might negotiate the complex social terrain" (2004, p. 22). Rarely do young black men let down their guard, to listen and to share their most intimate and personal reflections about their lives, yet in their doing so, we learn a great deal about what constitutes manhood.

The space that created these conversations is equally important when personal experiences and political consciousness converge. Political ideas often were woven throughout discussions during the weekly sessions to help the young men contextualize the ideas they would raise. For example, if someone said that his father was lazy for not working, the facilitator would ask about where all the jobs in Oakland had gone. MECA was more than a support group; it was also a pathway for these young black men to develop a political understanding of gender and act in ways that supported new understanding of black manhood.

FROM CRITICAL CONSCIOUSNESS TO ACTION: ACTIVISM AND BLACK MASCULINITY

These conversations were not only personal reflections, but also political education. The reflections of their fathers were entryways into understanding the social, political, and economic realities in their lives. Bilal was an important reason why these young men felt open and safe to share with each other. He was respected, and the young men knew that he had a similar story to their own. Bilal was what Akom (2006) refers to as a "new old head," an older man who spends time with youth in barbershops, malls, and basketball courts where youth congregate, to provide guidance. In some cases, the new old heads may have been formerly incarcerated, but got out the hustle and now spit game to youngstas who are hungry for another way of living. These are not exactly the new old heads whom Anderson describes in his ethnography of the Northton community: Anderson describes a man who

> feels hardly any obligation to his string of women and the children he has fathered. In fact he considers it a measure of success if he can get away with not being held legally accountable. . . . For him women are so many conquests, whose favors are obtained by "running a game." . . . Self-aggrandizement consumes his whole being. . . . On the corner he attempts to influence others by displaying the trappings of success. (1990, pp. 103–104)

The new old heads at MECA were more closely aligned with Akom's discussion of old heads, who are usually 30-something African American working-class males who are not gangbangers or drug dealers. Yet "[his] occupation as a hustler—a person who defies traditional social norms by sometimes working outside the formal economy, often without the privilege of possessing mainstream educational credentials—places him squarely on the bottom of the new urban economy" (2006, p. 82). Akom departs from Anderson's conceptualization of new old heads and argues that old heads care about young black men and impart life lessons at Raider games and on fishing trips and have influence and respect that are rooted in caring, not intimidation. Old heads use command of both black and standard English, hip-hop styles of dress, knowledge of local history, and a personal journey of surviving the streets that have earned them respect among Oakland's black youth.

For example, one night the young men were discussing a recent movie, *American Gangster*. The young men celebrated Frank Lucas, the main character, for his ruthless, shrewd business practices. Bilal simply asked, "How did Frank Lucas help or hurt the black community?" and "Is that the type of man you want to be?" Without telling young people how to think, his questions sparked discussions about their perceptions of manhood. Questioning was also supported by lessons about masculinity, sexism, misogyny, and power. When Vince first participated in the MECA support group, he held some of the strongest sexist views about women. It wasn't until he was confronted, and constantly challenged, by Bilal and other young men that his views about women began to change. He commented:

> My definition of what it meant to be a man was contorted because before coming to MECA I figured being a man was like how much money was in your pockets. So if I'm a man, I got to have the biggest stacks. I have to crack on anybody who is in my way to get what I need which was defined by how much I got in my pocket.

Vince began to develop a new understanding of manhood through conversations during MECA, reinforced by Bilal's constantly questioning, and discussing problematic views about manhood with the group. Bilal was not simply teaching these young men about manhood in formal lessons from a book, but modeled the behavior in his daily life. "In order for me to reach these youngstas, I have to be 'bout it! I can't tell them something like black women are queens, then turn around and call a woman a bitch. I have to live what I want to see in them. I have to believe it, live it, and be it." His strong commitment to embodying a worldview of justice was contagious among these young men who attended MECA. The young men began to correct each other when they used terms like "nigga," by simply saying to the person who used the term, "Oh, you mean 'brotha,' right?" Similarly, in regard to gender, the young men in the group began to reshape their language in ways that reflected a deeper consciousness about women and sexism. Vince commented about his own process of becoming conscious of sexism:

> I had a real problem with disrespecting women. Bilal would always call me out and check me when I was thinking about a woman in a disrespectful way. Like if a woman was speaking or something, I wouldn't give a fuck because I would be looking at her ass or something. I would be sitting hearing her talk, but thinking she got a big ass. But now when a woman speaks, I listen to her opinion, I want to know what she has to say. Bilal and this group brought me

out the little world that I was in and showed me what a man is suppose to be.

Bilal's solid connections with these young men allowed for him to challenge and confront them in ways that were stern, but caring. He understood that building political consciousness was like tending a vegetable garden. If nurtured and cared for over time, eventually it would yield an abundant harvest of food. When the young men would use negative terms, like "nigga," he wouldn't chastise them; rather, he would say, "Come on brotha's, we can use better terms for each other, let's see if you can use another way to talk about black people." Statements like these allowed for these young men to make mistakes and gently guided them back on track with constant reminders from Bilal. Over a period of a few months, Vince's ideas about manhood dramatically changed. He began to understand the ways in which personal experiences and the social world influenced his ideas of manhood in ways that would reproduce inequality and injustice. Vince discussed one small change about his perception of manhood:

> I used to want all these materials things like a gold chain because I felt like I needed to be seen. You know the gold chain really made me shine because I had nothing else to value. When I put on the gold chain, I was instantly somebody because I have this $300 chain. I felt superior like I mattered. But Bilil broke the mold and told me all that bullshit does not make you a man. He would say, "A real man comes from within, not from what you wear." So I applied that idea to all other types of things in my life, like a real man doesn't drag his family down or his community down so I applied that to what I was doing and robbing folks, selling dope. I stopped because I realized that a man doesn't hurt his own people, he uplifts them.

Bilal used multiple ways of hammering home the same message to the young men during Meca. He would have them read passages from the *Autobiography of Malcolm X*, passages from Huey P. Newton, bell hooks, the Willie Lynch letter, and other readings that he believed could further the young men's political consciousness. He often explained to the young men that critical consciousness was the only way to achieve freedom and liberation. During one session, he asked the young men if they had ever seen the movie *The Matrix*. Enthusiastically they recited scenes and recalled the film's amazing special effects. Without trying to silence their excitement about the movie, Bilal asked them what the "story" was about, not the movie. Some of the young men replied, "It's about them getting to

Zion," and "The movie is about using their special powers to defeat the Sentinels." One said that "It is a love story between Neo and Trinity—that's why he comes back to life." With excitement they all discussed their favorite scenes in the movie. Bilal explained to them that "the real story in *The Matrix* is about truth." Confused, they asked him to explain what he meant. He said, "What if I could show you that *The Matrix* is not simply a movie, but is real and that we are all influenced by it every moment of our lives? The real matrix," he explained, "is domination by one group over another with the consent of the group being dominated. The most powerful thing about the real matrix is that it tells people that it does not exist!" He pointed at a pair of expensive shoes one of the young men was wearing. Through intricate discussion about their desire for expensive shoes, he explained that those who created and manufactured the shoes controlled and created the youth's desire for the shoes for the long-term financial benefit of mostly wealthy adults.

He used this discussion to uncover the conceptual terrain that sociologists refer to as hegemony, domination by one group with the consent of the dominated group. The point of his illustration was to show how their behavior, attitudes, and choices were controlled but made to appear to be natural, without the influence of historical, contemporary, economic, social, and cultural forces. With a consciousness of how their lives are constrained by these forces, they can resist these forms of domination and actively make choices, "outside of the matrix." But first, they must better understand the contours of the matrix and how domination works in their lives. Discussions like these transformed the young men's political consciousness and encouraged them to "wake up" from oppressive ways of thinking about masculinity and compelled them to hold antisexist views of women.

WHO'S YOUR DADDY?

MECA had changed the views that some young black males held about masculinity and sexist views of women. Many of the young men corrected themselves when they used terms like "chick" and "shorty" to describe young women. Just as Marcus began to integrate the lessons at MECA, he had another challenge waiting for him at home. Turns out that his mother had agreed to let Reggie, his 10-year-old cousin, move in with them because Reggie's mother had got into trouble with the law again. Marcus wanted to try to teach Reggie some of the lessons he had learned at MECA. Reggie had started to hang out in the streets and was headed down the wrong path. Marcus, having already gone down that path, saw it as his responsibility to steer Reggie back in the right direction.

Marcus explained that he felt a responsibility to mentor and guide his cousin because if he didn't provide guidance, other young men in the streets would mentor him. Knowing that Reggie had few positive role models in his life, Marcus decided that he would take on the task of mentoring Reggie.

> I really took that chance to step out there and guide him in the right direction. I'm taking an initiative because I know he doesn't have a role model. I am his role model whether he likes it or not because he is living with us. So, I make sure I live up to my responsibilities. I give him the right information so he can make positive choices. I really have to make sure that I don't contradict myself and be a hypocrite. It's really making me step up to the plate.

Marcus takes Reggie to football practices during the week and to his games on Saturday morning. He checks his homework every night to make sure everything is correct. This was difficult for Marcus, given that he didn't care much for school. His mother and father had taught him the importance of school at an early age. Despite his own difficulties with school, however, Marcus worked with Reggie to help him with his homework. He also would take him to the store to buy supplies for his science projects and would make sure he had a lunch prepared before he left for school in the morning.

> You know, I'm always on him about his homework. My mom was always on me about my homework. I tell Reggie that he can't play sports if his grades aren't good. He can't have anything without his homework and doing good in school. So basically, I'm just reinforcing what my mom has already planted in me and that's being on your work. As far as sports, football, basketball, and everything, I support him a hundred percent but his school is first.

Marcus understood how important it was for Reggie to have a positive role model in his life. He also knew that Reggie respected him for listening and taking him to football and basketball practice. He explained that they had a big-brother type of relationship. But sometimes he felt more like a surrogate father to Reggie, particularly at times like Father's Day. Reggie would get into fights at school when his friends teased him because he didn't know his father. Marcus explained to Reggie, "Okay, I'm not your father, but I am like your big brother." This was enough for Reggie to feel better because he would return to school the next day and show Marcus to all his friends on the playground. It was enough for Marcus to feel like he made a difference in Reggie's life.

Marcus also uses many of the lessons he had learned during MECA to support Reggie. Remembering how it felt to be silenced by his mother and father, he remembered a night during MECA when the young men talked about how they wanted to improve communication with their parents. Many of them felt that their parents simply didn't listen to them. Marcus remembered the discussion and wanted to avoid silencing Reggie. During one of their disagreements, he asked Reggie to list everything he didn't like about him so they could discuss it openly. Marcus felt that it was better to talk openly than for Reggie to harbor ill feeling toward him.

> Sometimes we don't give kids a chance to say what is on their mind. They say things behind closed doors and don't say it to your face. So I tell Reggie, "I want you to be up front with me. If there's a problem that you have, tell me. Communicate with me." So he told me that sometimes I didn't listen to him. I started to think, damm that's just what I felt like with my mom and dad! So I told myself that I needed to start listening to him more. I have to start letting him voice his opinions sometimes. Sometimes I just shut it off like I'm authority and that's it. When I was a kid, I didn't want to be shut up like that. I had to put myself in his shoes for second. When we talked and I put myself in his situation, it gave me a whole another point of view. He just wanted me to listen to him a little more and hear him out about things he's going through.

Marcus's perspective of manhood wasn't perfect. He sometimes used terms for women he knew were sexist. He also learned from the young men who attended MECA that consciousness didn't happen overnight, but developed over time. The time Marcus spent with his cousin Reggie illustrates that critical consciousness can change how young black men view fatherhood. By spending time with Reggie, Marcus contributed to his own growth and development as well. Their relationship represented a perspective of black young men as caring, gentle, and loving, a perspective that is unfortunately rarely depicted. Marcus's consciousness about black men, and his new understanding of masculinity, encouraged him to care for his cousin and mentor him through difficult times.

Marcus's mentoring of his cousin represents personal dimensions of activism that require intensely personal reflection, and small actions that ultimately make a big difference. His experiences in MECA ultimately transformed his understanding of fatherhood, which encouraged him to take responsibility for raising his cousin. It is true that few young black men would make the same choice to raise, mentor, and guide a younger sibling or cousin. It is likely that there are other variables that contributed to Marcus's commitment. However, support, dialogue, and critical consciousness about his life compelled him to do the same for others.

VINCE'S HOMECOMING

After a few months, Vince mentioned to the group that he wanted to see if he could get over the hatred that he held for not having his father in his life. He wanted to go up to the county jail, where he had recently heard that his father was incarcerated, and tell him how he felt about not having him around. Another young man in the group confirmed that he too wanted the opportunity to meet his father and confront him about not having him in his life. Bilal suggested that they go up to jail and that nothing was holding them back from doing what they wanted to do. Vince took Bilal's advice and found out when he could visit the jail and talk to his father. Taking one of the most courageous steps of his life, he placed his name on the visitor list at the jail and wrote his father's name next to his.

> I just had to see him, his face, and I wanted to see his reaction when I told him that I was Dorothy's son, his son. At first he didn't really know who I was until I told him. The first thing he said to me was, "You done grown up so fast!" I thought to myself, don't hold back, tell him exactly what I want him to know. So I said to him, "How would you know, you never were around to see me!" He just sort of sat there, when I said that. I told him how much he hurt me for not being there. I told him I wished he was around to show me how to knot my tie on prom night, I wanted him to tell me to run faster at my football practices, I wanted him to get on me for not doing my homework! You know, all that kind of shit. I got emotional and started to cry because I was so angry at him, I wanted him to know how much he hurt me and my family.

Vince's father didn't respond with excuses, blaming his mother, or blaming the system, the way Vince had anticipated. What his father told him shook him to the core. Vince would have preferred hearing the excuses, rather than how his father responded. His father looked directly into his eyes and said in a low, sincere voice that he was so very sorry for causing him and his mother so much pain. "Nothing I can say or do will ever heal that, I did y'all wrong and I'll have to live with that for the rest of my life. But you, Vince, can make another choice and not to repeat the mistakes I made." Vince wasn't ready to hear that from his father. He was prepared for excuses from his father and would have preferred a heated confrontation with him. Instead, he saw his father shed tears right in front of him for the pain he had caused. The encounter was overwhelming. They both cried; they shed tears without words, not knowing what to say, but feeling they were headed in the right direction.

Vince returned to MECA with a new sense of accomplishment. He had done what he had only imagined; he confronted his father and began reconciling their relationship. The other young men were so intrigued by what Vince had done, a flurry of questions derailed the scheduled topic for the evening. "What did he say to you, Vince?" "How did you get into the visiting hours?" "Did he know who you were?" "Did you curse him out?" One by one, Vince responded to the questions as Bilal and the other youth listened with intensity. Vince realized that his encounter with his father was more than his own individual healing; his act of courage also opened the door for his father to heal as well. He returned to the jail the following week, and upon seeing Vince, his father smiled and was glad to see him again. They talked about why he had not been around; they laughed at small things Vince remembered about his father when he did see him. Like the time his father gave him a sip of beer, when his mother wasn't looking. After several weeks of these meetings his father confessed to him that there were "a lot of guys in here who would love to do this. You know, talk with children they didn't do right by, but they scared, Vince, they don't know what to say or where to start." Sometimes ideas emerge from the spirit over long periods of time; other times ideas are summoned with lightning speed. Vince felt a sense of inspiration, fear, and concern that he had never experienced before. But something deep inside him told him that he needed to connect more incarcerated fathers with their children.

Vince didn't know what to expect on the 1st day they held the meeting with incarcerated fathers and their children at the jail. He would have been pleased if three or four men attended, despite all the work and time organizing the session required. Maneuvering visiting hours, mealtimes, instructional classes, and permissions from the jail's warden, however, was not as difficult as he had anticipated with Bilal's help and guidance. When he walked into the room Vince was surprised to find all 20 of the chairs filled with men wanting to reconcile their relationships with their children, and to hear their children share their stories. Vince remarked:

> I can't really describe the feeling to know that this was happening because of something I did. Meeting my father changed my life because when I released all the hate that I was holding it was like there was more space for positive things to come in my life.

Meeting his father allowed him to release all that he had been holding, and by letting go of his pain and anger, he was able to act on behalf of others. Every Tuesday at 6:00 p.m., the group met to hear from fathers, and their children. The rules for these meetings were simple: Everyone sit in a circle, let people share their own story, no blaming others, and tell the truth. Vince had learned from Bilal that everyone had a story to tell. Some stories were profound, some ordinary. But giving people the opportunity to testify and bear witness to their stories was a powerful healing tool, which if supported in community can transform our spirits and open up new possibilities for our lives and the lives of others.

Vince's homecoming was more than a reconciliation with his father. Rather, it illustrates how the convergence of the personal and political domains of civic life contribute to activism. For Vince, creating the father's group was not simply an individual act driven by personal motivation, but an example of new conceptions of masculinity and agency.

Mutua's (2006) notion of masculinity suggests that progressive black masculinities must promote human freedom, embrace dignity, and celebrate justice. For young black men, remaking masculinity in ways that promote healing, justice, and freedom are significant because this process resists negative images of black men and recasts the images in ways that more accurately reflect the fears and dreams, the doubts and imagination of young black men's lives. Masculinity in this respect must be directed at liberation not only from structural barriers that stand in the way of mobility, but also from psychosocial chains that limit the capacity to heal and stand in the way of healing for others.

This notion of masculinity offers us a new dimension of activism and another entry point into civic engagement for African American youth. The process involves building the capacity to heal from personal and social issues, developing young people's political consciousness to help them understand the root causes of these issues, and preparing them to act in ways that changes personal and social problems. Martin Sánchez-Jankowski (2002) reminds us that we need a more nuanced understanding of civic life for youth who have histories of experiencing racial discrimination, personal trauma, and exclusion from mainstream civic activities. Through progressive ideas about masculinity, these young men were able to reengage in community life in ways that were consistent with their new beliefs about manhood.

5

Reclaiming Africa: Building Racial Wellness Among African American Youth

BUILDING HEALTHY RACIAL and ethnic identities among African American youth is an important aspect of the healing process. In a society where African identity is devalued and demeaned, the radical healing process must consider the ways to rebuild and reclaim racial identity among African American youth. One central theme throughout this book has been that youth workers, policy makers, and teachers must find ways to cultivate youth activism by focusing on ways to build upon the strengths of black youth. These strengths are sometimes hidden just beneath the surface of their identities and can be cultivated by exposure to new ways of seeing the world. A healthy racial identity is one way that African American youth can foster a new worldview.

However, there is a constant threat to healthy identity formation for African American youth. Negative beliefs about blackness are so deeply woven into the psychic fabric of American culture that it becomes difficult for African American young people to appreciate a healthy African identity. I have often discussed this idea with African American youth by asking them to describe to me the difference between "good hair and bad hair." Typically, youth respond by saying, "Good hair is easy to comb through, smooth and silky, whereas bad hair is kinky and hard to comb." In some instances, students have demonstrated to me the difference by pointing out students in the room with "good hair" and others with "bad hair." The point that I illustrate to young people is that hair cannot be good or bad any more than skin can be good or bad. The only difference is the meaning we assign to differences in hair texture. These meanings have been prescribed and are formed by historical and contemporary ideas of blackness. Commercials, TV advertisements, and even intraracial jokes like "You're so black that . . ."—all are internalized forms of racism and contribute to damaging beliefs about black identity. However, when young people are made aware of how racism influences how they see themselves, they resist and seek new and empowering images of themselves. For example, they choose to wear their hair in locks or in a more natural state. Others may change their names to reflect their African culture. Identity formation and the choices that young people make are embedded within a sociopolitical context and are constrained by racial, gender, and economic oppression (Robinson & Ward, 1992). Fostering a consciousness of these forces among youth by illustrating how they internalize these ideas provides them with a powerful critical perspective, or "oppositional gaze," about their social world and their place in it. This critical awareness is important in developing the type of resistance in which black youth are encouraged to "acknowledge the problems, and to demand change, in an environment that oppresses them" (Robinson & Ward, 1992, p. 89). Research generally distinguishes between two types of resistance among African American youth. The first is oppositional resistance, short-term forms of resistance that foster "self-denigration due to the internalization of negative self image, excessive autonomy and individualism at the expense of connectedness to the collective" (p. 89). Oppositional resistance has been widely used to explain school failure, delinquent behavior, and violence (Fordham, 1996; Ogbu, 1990; Willis, 1977). Oppositional resistance can be conceptualized as a set of shared values, beliefs, and attitudes that reject dominant social norms and contribute to behaviors that make it difficult to achieve. The second is transformative resistance, where black youth are "encouraged to acknowledge the problems of, and to demand change in, an environment that oppresses them" (Robinson & Ward, p. 88). This form of resistance encourages black youth to reject toxic images and beliefs about blackness and redefine black identity in a way that is self-critical and culturally affirming. Transformative resistance is an important aspect of black youth political behavior because it is often shaped by deeply personal challenges such as pregnancy, shame of racial identity, or traumatic experiences. Transformative resistance is precisely the capacity to cultivate and sustain what Melucci (1988) called "submerged networks" of everyday political life where actors produce and practice alternative frameworks of meaning, social relations, and collective identity below the horizon of established or officially recognized institutions" (Gregory, 1998). While youth (under the ages of 18) cannot vote, have little power to change policies and laws, and have limited access to institutional politics, transformative resistance is often spawned through attempts to confront personal challenges in their lives. Unlike oppositional resistance, which views resistance as contributing to educational failure and a host of youth problems, transformative resistance is linked to social change and allows black youth to reject self-blame for personal problems and fosters a critical worldview that is informed by their particular social, economic, and political position.

A central component of transformative resistance is to recover an identity that protects black youth from constant racial stigmatization and sustains a positive sense of belonging to a vibrant, significant, and meaningful African culture. Building transformative resistance means that African American youth build their identities in ways that connect them to a broader struggle for racial justice, which can provide meaning and purpose to their lives. Transformative resistance, in this sense, is a healthy psychosocial response to oppression and, while undertheorized, an important aspect in the youth development process. Resistance can be viewed as a type of psychic armor that prepares young people to confront racism while at the same time embracing a black identity with personal and communal life-affirming meaning. Efforts to promote personal and collective liberation requires a self-conscious process that allow young people to challenge the structural and systemic barriers by drawing upon the strengths of one's history and cultural connection.

This chapter describes how culture can build transformative resistance among black youth. In 1999, Leadership Excellence designed a 2-weeks-abroad program in Ghana called Camp Akebulan. Consistent with all the programming at Leadership Excellence, the program was designed to build critical consciousness through exposure to African culture. This chapter identifies how exposure to cultural experiences connected them to a broader struggle for justice. Upon return from Ghana, the youth reflected on their experiences and took up new forms of activism directed at racial justice and improving the quality of life for all African people. This chapter focuses on two of the youth who participated in the 2-week trip to Ghana— Lateefa, an 18-year-old student and mother, and Tré, a 16-year-old young man who was referred to Leadership Excellence by his mother's church.

RETURN TO HOME: CAMP AKEBULAN AND YOUTH IDENTITY

Selecting the 15 youth who participated in the organization's first trip to Africa was not an easy task. The staff had prepared a rigorous 1-year-long preparation course that involved learning about the history of Ghana, cultural-awareness activities, and weekly fund-raising events. The youth who were finally selected were not the typical academically strong students. In fact the staff were intentional about not "creaming" youth and therefore only selecting the students whom we knew would do well. Some students were in group homes, others lived with grandparents, and some attended school regularly. The coordinators of the program had anticipated that only 15 youth out of 40 would complete the rigorous tasks and assignments that were required to participate in Camp Akebulon. First, each student had to raise $1,000 to match the $2,000 per person that had been raised by grants and donors from Learning Excellence staff. Second, each student needed to attend weekly cultural-history lessons and activities that would prepare them for the trip. Third, they needed to follow through on logistical requirements such as obtaining a visa and passport and getting the required shots.

Despite all the challenges, 15 youth completed all the requirements and were presented with their tickets to Ghana. In August 1999, we all boarded the airplane for a 20-hour trip to Ghana, excited and nervous about what was to come. Several of the young people had never traveled outside California, so we were not surprised when we landed in New York a few hours after leaving San Francisco that many of the young people were excited to be in New York at JFK Airport. We probably didn't realize at the time the profound impact that this trip would have on our lives. When we landed in Accra, Ghana, we stepped out of the plane onto Ghana's deep-red soil and saw hundreds of loving black faces waiting for us. We were changed forever.

Leadership Excellence staff described their trip to Accra as more than a tour or cultural exchange, but rather as a pilgrimage meant to reconnect them to a culture that had been severed from their past. As we loaded onto the bus at the airport in Ghana headed toward the University of Legon, faces were pressed close to the window looking out as if we were searching the crowded streets for long-lost cousins. Kenda, a 16-year-old youth from West Oakland, commented, "This feels like going to my cousin's house in Mississippi, the trees, the people and even the heat feels like Biloxi!" There was indeed something familiar about the sweet, humid air, and as we settled into our dorm rooms at the University of Legon, the young people took out their journals to document their reflections about being in Ghana. What follows are two young people's reflections about the experience of going to Ghana for the first time.

LATEEFA'S STORY: FROM WEST OAKLAND TO WEST AFRICA AND BACK

Lateefa grew up in West Oakland and, at 17-years-old, cares for her two children, aged 2 and 6; holds down a job; and struggles with trying to complete school. When she was about 15, she began selling drugs with her boyfriend and began prostituting for him in order to support his growing drug addiction. According to Lateefa, young prostitutes are more common than people realize. She said, "When girls have a young man in their life and they really care about them, they have to lower themselves to his level to bring him up out of the gutter. . . . Yeah, I gotta sell drugs, I gotta sell my body for him." Lateefa rarely discussed these painful experiences with anyone and frequently turned to poetry to deal with the feelings and experiences from her childhood. She now works part time at Old Navy in a nearby city and has decided that she wants to go on to college.

Lateefa's green eyes; golden, light skin; and jet black hair are clear markers of her biracial identity, which has made it difficult for her to fit into racial categories. "I have African and Puerto Rican blood in me, so I hung out with all the Mexicans. But the black girls didn't like me because I hung out with the Mexicans, and the Mexicans didn't like me because I looked darker than them." Despite speaking fluent Spanish, she could not find an easy entrée into the Hispanic clique at school.

Going to Africa for Lateefa was an opportunity for her to learn about her African roots and become more rooted in both her ethnic identities. Almost immediately after arriving in Accra, Lateefa began to learn about herself in unexpected ways. Her adjustment to a different way of life was not easy, and as a result, the first few days of her trip was difficult for her. She complained about the food, the tight sleeping quarters, and the heat, and she hated riding on the crowded buses. I talked with her several times and she explained to me that she wanted to go home, and despite having prepared for the trip, it was not what she had expected. She explained,

> I'm not feeling this whole trip thing to Africa! I know every body is like, "Let Lateefa go back home, because she getting on our nerves complaining about everything." But I am not feeling it! Why did I fly all this way to get bit by mosquitoes, ride with these funky people, and eat this nasty food! I am sorry, but I am not feeling this.

Having never traveled outside California, Lateefa didn't know what to expect. Traveling abroad simply intensified her nervousness and anxiety about being in unfamiliar surroundings. She also knew that sending her back to Oakland was not an option because we had already explained to the parents and guardians the risks of sending a youth home from West Africa alone. It wasn't until we attended a large outdoor market in Accra, 3 days after we arrived, that she began to settle into the trip and learn new things about herself. Her journal entry illustrated this:

> The other day at the market this guy was trying to sell me a bag of apples or something. I told him, no I don't want to buy an apple. He continued to ask me again and I was getting angry because he

wouldn't stop, he just kept trying to sell me these apples. He was like, "You want an apple"? I told him no hella times, but then he reached in the bag and sliced some up in fours, and said, "You want a slice of an apple?" I couldn't believe it! I knew he understood what I was saying, but he continued to slice up the apples and ask me if I wanted to buy the slices. I realized he was just trying to get his hussle on and trying to make his money so he could survive for that day. That really made me kinda think about how easy it is for me to make money at home and how hard they have it in Ghana. I thought, I don't really do much to earn money, and the job that I do have I complain and say, "God why do I have to do this?" My job at home is not even that bad. Yet he has to sell apples, and if he can't sell an apple, he has to sell slices of an apple just to live for that day. Like, they don't complain about stuff, and I'm constantly complaining, I want to do this and I want to do that. They're just beautiful people. And I'm black too, I'm African too, so why aren't I acting like them? Why am, why do I complain about stuff? Is it because the way I was taught?

Lateefa's insight about how Ghanaian youth struggled with poverty forced her to understand things she took for granted in Oakland. She also began to reflect on why her behavior and attitudes were so different from those of the Ghanaian youth she encountered. She had witnessed firsthand the profound impact of poverty in Ghana. Yet she also was struck by the sense of pride and grace Ghanaians possessed. Lateefa and the other young people on the trip every night shared similar stories and would discuss them during our nightly debriefing dinners. After a week, Lateefa's outlook was entirely different from that of her first few days in Ghana. During one of our dinners, she remarked:

I have not been here very long and I am already learning so much. I mean, I've changed a little bit already. You know, I have never been out of the state of California before and here I am in Africa! Just seeing the faces that are like mine, and so beautiful, I feel like I want to live here someday because the people here are so poor, but they are proud and strong! I wonder if this is where Mom gets her strength from, am I strong like my African sisters? I wonder if we gotta deal with some of the same issues?

Most days the young people visited schools, recreation centers, and markets, museums and festivals. For Lateefa, spending time with Ghanaian youth to discuss issues like education, hip-hop music, dance clubs, and work marked a dramatic shift in her consciousness about herself and her own ethnic identity. She explained that one day she was walking with a Ghanaian high school student near the university when everything changed for her:

> We were walking back to the dorms when something triggered like, "Damn, I'm in Africa!" We kept talking about things that bothered me about the United States, and things she [the Ghanaian student] wanted to know about Oakland. But it finally hit me that I was really in Africa and how much I was learning. I realized that our family was here, and they were taken from here on chains, in a boat. It took me a while to actually think about! But I realized that here I'm standing in this actual place where all this shit started and where it actually happened. It also occurred to me that I'm here by choice. I can leave if I want to, I can come and leave when I want to, no one is going to handcuff me. I'm here and I was just feeling the whole thing! I could feel the spirits just looking at me smiling! That was tight, I was really feeling that situation, really feeling it!

As Lateefa shared her story with us over dinner, her eyes were filled with excitement as if she had just discovered a gold mine. As she shared her story, the other young people were surprised to learn that she had learned so much and was now excited about the trip. But her excitement was dampened by an incident that taught her about racial identity in Ghana. During the day, Lateefa, with a group of other girls from our group, were shopping when they were stopped by several little children who commented on Lateefa's hair and skin. "Your hair is so straight and your light skin is so pretty," the children commented. One of the little girls said, "I wish my skin was not dark, I think your skin is much prettier than mine and so is your hair." Their short thick hair and beautifully dark skin stood in stark contrast to Lateefa's straight black hair and caramel-tone skin. The other young women from our group just stood and watched as the Ghanaian children gawked at Lateefa's "European" features and ignored the other young women in the group.

This painful experience was not easy for Lateefa to talk openly about; neither was it easy for the other young women to discuss. The experience was a familiar reminder that black skin and African features were not valued, not even in Africa. During our conversation about this event later that evening, several youth commented about seeing numerous advertisements on billboards promoting skin bleaching. Lateefa also learned a great deal about her own identity from this experience. She commented that her blackness and African roots were more than simply surface, physical appearance, but were deeply spiritual and ancestral. Lateefa and the other young women vowed to celebrate their African features and reject ways that they have been taught to value beauty. After this encounter, several of the girls stayed up all night braiding their hair, and some of them discussed where they were going to get their hair locked when they returned to Oakland. "I want my locks to be groomed, and I'll have some of those cowrie shells on the ends." Their consciousness about African identity was not only limited to their appearance; they also developed a profound knowledge of the Asante people in Ghana and a solid understanding of the African slave trade. Unlike learning from a textbook in school, or concepts from a history course, the ideas and historical understanding of the African slave trade reshaped Lateefa's racial awareness and consciousness about her connections to Africa.

BUILDING KNOWLEDGE OF SELF IN A SLAVE DUNGEON

The trip from Accra to Cape Coast was long, hot, and dusty. The main road between the cities hadn't been repaved for years, and what would normally be a 3-hour drive took almost 8 hours. Our primary purpose for visiting Cape Coast was to participate in a reenactment of how West Africans were captured into the slave trade and endured the inhumane captivity in Elmina Castle dungeons. Lateefa was wearing traditional African clothing she had purchased at a local market, and the bright blues and burgundy seemed to glow as we all prepared for the tour of Elmina Castle. The tour of the castle was perfunctory, as we viewed the church, the courtyard, and the sailors' quarters. But as we entered the dungeons, we could hear drums from a distance and moaning and crying as we went into the dank, dark bowels of the castle. With only a torch lighting the way, they explained to us the horrors of being captured, placed in captivity for months waiting for the ship that would set sail for the new world. As we slowly descended into the dungeons, the thick, humid smell of suffering was nearly suffocating. The reenactment was almost too real. We were lined up and marched into dark holding cells where we were told that Africans had to endure these conditions for months until being loaded onto a ship. We were given vivid details about how Africans were forced to eat, sleep, and defecate in the same place where we were standing. For Lateefa and the other youth, this event played a significant role in their own identity development and helped them to understand that their culture was connected to a history of struggle.

> I really never really understood the slave trade but when I heard them talk about it today and show us how it happened, I really got angry at Europeans and Spanish for how they treated us. But also, I

didn't know that other Africans participated in the slave trade, that
shocked me because I didn't know about any of that.

When we went into the dungeon, I felt like it [being captured
into the slave trade] was actually happening to me. The darkness,
the hot air, and the smell almost made me sick, but I said if my
ancestors could survive this then I had to honor them by experiencing this. It's an experience that you don't realize what's happening
until you actually go through it. You know, actually being there on
the very ground and soil where our ancestors were captured. We all
were feeling like our ancestors were calling out to us. It was next
level to be in the place where all this actually happened. We were
there going through it, hearing the sounds, feeling the fear, and
feeling the vibes, just everything. It was so emotional I couldn't help
but break down and cry cuz I finally knew what they went through,
sacrificed for me to be here.

Lateefa was not alone in her realization about the suffering of her
African ancestors. We concluded the reenactment with the sound of chains
and finally the loud thud of the "door of no return," opened to the furious
swells of the Atlantic Ocean. Three young men held on tight to each other
as they fought their futile efforts to hold back their tears. "After the Africans passed through this door out of the dungeon onto the slave ships"
the tour guide warned, "they would never see their homeland again. This
is the door of no return."

The visit to Elmina awakened the young people's consciousness about
the history of triumph and struggle for Africans throughout the world. For
Lateefa, her identity was not simply relegated to a few facts about Africa
in a history book, but rather was redefined to encompass an entire history,
experience, and legacy that was, until this point in her life, disconnected
from her day-to-day life. Now she understood that she was African, and
that made all the difference in the world.

We could have taken a trip anywhere, but it would not have an impact on us. I would not have been as into the trip because we wouldn't
have felt it. Going on this trip helped me get a grip on reality, things I
didn't even know. Like if we would gone to Paris, it's not gonna help
us because we are not from Europe. Now Africa, our ancestors were
from here, we were stolen from here, and we've come back! We're
Africans, you know, and we're back in Africa, where we belong.

Lateefa's identification with Africa marked a significant shift in her
racial and ethnic identity. Her African identity not only served as a pow-

erful antidote to confront years of negative images of blackness, but her identity was also a new space to see new possibilities for herself and an opening for her to envision a compelling future. In many ways, this experience for Lateefa forced her to see herself connected to a deep and rich legacy of struggle and triumph. Other youth had similar experiences. Her identity was bigger than she could have ever imagined, which rooted her to a place, a people, and a purpose.

> It was painful, going into the dungeon and walking down that long tunnel. They told us how many Africans they stuffed into that one cell; it was too much! It made me wonder, "How can people do that to another race?" Afterward it made me think about how blacks need to be paid back for all that was done to us. We built the United States and they still haven't gave us the credit that we deserve. For me that experience broadened my horizons; it opened my eyes to the fact that, that I'm just a small person in this world, and I've got so much to learn.

Lateefa's experience was not unique. Other young people on the trip experienced their own struggles and triumphs in different ways. For some, simply being away from the familiar surroundings of Oakland for so long made the trip difficult. For others, eating unfamiliar food or sleeping in crowded quarters raised their own levels of tolerance and forced them to value the things they had taken for granted. We had no idea, however, that these issues would be relatively minor to one we were about to confront.

TRE'S STORY

Tre hadn't hit a blunt in nearly 2 weeks since leaving Oakland and he was craving his next high. Despite agreeing to the rules to not bring or possess drugs, and being warned about the threat of being jailed in a Ghanaian prison for possessing drugs, Tre found a way to smuggle several joints into his suitcase. Tre's distinctive Oakland accent, baggy pants, and gold chains made him stand out when we traveled in Ghana. At 6 feet, Tre towered over all the other youth on the trip and, despite his skinny frame, his baby face made him look much younger than 16. Tre was always quiet and polite and in the 3 years since he had begun Leadership Excellence's programs, he had never posed any serious problems. On a warm afternoon in Cape Coast after a nice dinner, one of the adult counselors commented that Tre had been missing for about an hour and upon his return, she thought that he might be high. I approached him, only to confirm her suspicions. His eyes were red and the smell of marijuana clung to his clothing. The conversation with him was surprisingly easy. He confessed to smoking and explained that it was no big deal. He knew as well as I did that we could not send him home—the complexity, difficulty, and cost of traveling back to California alone were too great. We decided that his violation was not simply a matter of rules, but that he had violated the trust of the entire group and ruptured the vibe and energy that we had developed over the past 2 weeks. As a result, the entire group would need to decide how to proceed with this dilemma.

We called a "family meeting" with everyone in the entire group to discuss the situation and figure out how to move forward. After I explained the situation to the group, I asked Tre to explain to everyone what happened. The group asked him to account for his behavior, speak about how his actions affected them and the group, and talk about how his behavior could affect the organization. He surprisingly took responsibility for his actions without being prompted but was scolded by the other youth for putting the entire group in jeopardy and "disrespecting the vibe," as one of the youth put it. The conversation was rather difficult, because our previous family meetings were uplifting, and this was the first time we needed to discuss what to do with someone who had violated the rules. The young people suggested that he be restricted from the beach and nighttime activities. Something didn't feel right about punishment, so rather than looking for punishment, I asked how we could learn from Tre's actions and suggested that I call his mother and explain what happened. The experience of being responsible to the group, and having to discuss this with his mother upon our return, was consequence enough.

Our decision to focus on learning from mistakes, rather than distributing creative punishment, turned out to be a good one. Restricting Tre from the other activities could have neglected important learning opportunities for him. The following day, we all visited a small school in Cape Coast where youth in the group learned for the first time that schooling in Ghana was not free and that all school-aged children and youth had to work to pay for their tuition. Tre noted:

> I met Antwi, who is in 12th grade, who told me that he needed some money for his schoolbooks and stuff like that. I was like, "What do you mean you need money for books?" He explained that he works so that he can pay tuition for school. School was like the main thing for him and his friends and I was like, man, so that's how it should be back in the U.S.

In fact, our local guide informed us that unlike the United States where young people can find part-time work in fast food or retail, many of the young people in Cape Coast have to be creative to generate money. We learned that it was common for teenage boys to gather stones and crush them up to make gravel to be sold to contractors building homes in the area. Tre seemed to become more conscious of the difference in how his Ghanaian counterparts viewed their education.

> I was surprised to see even the little kids was really into their school, like it was a video game or something. It was like they saw school as being an adventure, almost life and death. That was eye opening to me because it's not like that in Oakland. It's like we just take school for granted, but here they soak it up here.

During our nightly debrief, Tre began to rethink some of the everyday things he took for granted back in Oakland. School, work, and food were things he did not think much about, but being here in Ghana and seeing how young people his own age struggled, opened his consciousness to a level of poverty that he hadn't known existed. After dinner one night, we noticed our Ghanaian guide gathering up the leftover food that we were throwing away and putting it in containers. Shortly thereafter, he took three neatly packed bags downstairs to 10 children who were eagerly waiting for him. Tre did know exactly how to feel and was at first angry at our guide for giving them "our scraps." When he asked our guide why he did this, the guide replied to Tre, "To you they may be scraps, but to us this is a meal which may not come as regularly as your meals do. We are careful not to waste even the smallest things." Tre ruminated on this:

> At first I was hella mad at him for giving them scraps. Then basically after he explained it, I felt privileged even though I am poor. I don't have jewelry, I'm not bling blingin' and everything and I don't have that much money. But what little I do have makes me damn near rich here.

The opportunity for Tre to reflect on his ethnic and class identity forced him to grapple with things that he once took for granted. Having his own room, playing with his Xbox at home, or chatting with his friends using his cell phone were experiences that he took for granted. Despite the fact that he lives in a poor working-class community in Oakland, his exposure to poverty in Ghana compelled him to make connections between poverty in the United States and how his Ghanaian counterparts struggled to make it.

Tre spent the following day with several of his newfound Ghanaian friends. He was amazed at how they built things to sell and used their artistic ability to earn money. His most profound understanding, however, came from knowing that his counterparts had few other options to survive. Tre commented during dinner one night:

> Man, they make everything here! Drums, artwork, take old tires and sell the rubber, take lead from car rims and sell the metal. Most of what they gotta do is make it with their bare hands. We are so used to paying somebody to build something, but here they go out and make it themselves to earn money. It's a whole other level of hustling because if they don't sell they don't eat.

His insights about poverty and struggling also influenced how he saw illegal street activities as not simply a hustle but a means to survive. The most significant difference between hustling in Ghana and hustling in Oakland, however, was that the Ghanaian youth he met did not sell drugs, whereas the Oakland youth rarely sold handmade goods. More important, he saw connections between the spirit of struggle from his Ghanaian friends and his friends in Oakland. He explained:

> When I see my partners on the street corner or a bunch of my brothers, what I see is a bunch of lost warriors. I see the brothas on the corner as the same Africans that I see here in Africa but the ones on the corner in Oakland are lost. What I mean by lost is, all those powers that I seen out here, hustling to survive, supporting each other, making stuff with your own hands are being used to sell drugs. We both hustling, selling what ever we can but they [Ghanaian youth] don't sell crack or heroine or anything like that. On the street corner, we are using our hustling skills to destroy ourselves. We are strong warriors but we are strong warriors out there in Oakland with guns and we are lost in the head by not knowing who we are so we take our anger out on the next brother who looks just like us.

Tre's insight about the connections between Ghanaian youth and his counterparts in Oakland broadened his consciousness about social justice. He began to understand that while there were profound differences in their respective experience of poverty, there were entirely different ways to resist and navigate unjust conditions. The young people in Ghana used their resources to create economic opportunities that contributed to broader civic and community life. Locating trees to cut down, gathering metals, carving statues all were collective activities where groups of young men would spend time together, sharing stories and exchanging information about their particular trade. Tre realized while the root cause of selling drugs in Oakland was the same reason that drove his Ghanaian counterparts to sell crafts in Accra, the outcomes for hustling were very different. Simply put, selling drugs destroyed African people, while selling crafts celebrated African culture. Tre stated:

> I noticed that a lot of things that we do in Oakland is similar to what they do in Ghana—it's all African. We play loud music, they play drums here. The loud beats in our car, the gold teeth, and the locks, that is all African traditions and culture. The dancing, every-thing we do is African. Even the sideshows [illegal street parties where youth show off their cars by spinning tires] we do in Oak-land, that's African too. Even though the Ghanaians don't spin cars like we do in Oakland, they gather lots of people together to cele-brate with music, drink, that's African. I really just started to think and connect things. So basically what it taught me was we have a lot of power being out in the streets. Our power came from Africa, but instead of using our power to build, we are using our power to destroy ourselves. But if you look at it right now, all the drugs they flooded us with, all the poverty, we went to slavery and we still surviving and thriving!

Lateefa's and Tre's lessons had a profound impact on their identity and political consciousness when they returned to Oakland. Our last day in Ghana was celebrated with a large farewell dinner complete with drum-ming and a naming ceremony where each of us were given traditional Ghanaian names. Some of us boarded the plane with mixed emotions, feel-ing that by finding our African selves we received so much more than we gave. The fruit from these seeds would blossom not on Ghana's shores, but in Oakland streets.

BLACKNESS ON THE BLOCK: RETURNING TO OAKLAND

The trip to Ghana for many of the young people served as a key turning point in their identity development and the maturation of their political consciousness. The ability to experience and connect with Ghanaians left an indelible mark on their worldview and nurtured a vision for their own place in the world. Some of the young women expressed their newfound identity by wearing their hair naturally in locks or braids rather than straightening their hair, signaling their appreciation of African identity. Others wore their African attire and necklaces, signifying their newly discovered African consciousness. Their identity and political consciousness came to play a central role in the forms and content of their activism.

Lateefa had returned to Oakland with a new sense of optimism and eagerness to complete school and eventually go on to college. Her optimism, however, was not without challenges. Shortly after her return to Oakland, she learned that she was pregnant. While this situation could have forced her to simply give up and return to the streets, her empowered identity as an African woman and her political consciousness encouraged her to understand how intensely personal struggles and political issues influence her life. The well-known adage from the women's rights movement "The personal is political" exemplifies how the trip to Ghana for Lateefa cultivated an understanding that personal issues often have political explanations.

Upon learning that she was pregnant, she went to sign up for a free child-care center at her school that allowed for parenting mothers to complete school without having to drop out in order to care for their children.

> I had my baby in March and the school had a program that provided child care so that I could still go to school and graduate. When I went to sign up for the free child-care program, they told me that the child care center would not be open because there were not enough girls signed up. Now this leaves me without child care, and I cannot go to summer school. I don't have anybody to watch my child, I don't have any money to pay for child care, which is $135 a week! I don't have that kind of money. I told them, "What do you expect me to do?" I'm not going to be one of those African American teen mother statistics you know, I am going to graduate from high school.

Lateefa's political consciousness encouraged her to conceptualize the closure of the center as a denial of her and other pregnant students' right to access to education. By challenging the district's decision to close the center, she also conceptualized the closure as dismissing black pregnant girls as statistics and as people who were not interested in graduating anyway. Her ethnic and racial identity also influenced how she viewed her situation as act of injustice toward black parenting teens. During a Leadership Excellence meeting, Lateefa explained her situation to us:

> I told the people at the district that I'm gonna try my hardest to get this day care open, and if I don't get this day care open, I will find people who help me and assist me to open the day care for summer

school for teen parents. You know, this situation is harder for me to deal with because I'm young; you adults are out of school, you have jobs, you have a family. I haven't reached that point yet, I'm still trying to get out of high school. How can you stop someone who is trying to improve, you know?

Lateefa shared her personal challenge (being pregnant) with other youth in the context of a larger political discussion about black youth issues in Oakland. During the discussion, other youth shared stories about how their rights were denied by other public institutions. Lateefa's political consciousness influenced her understanding of the closure of the school as a political issue, rather than a personal problem. Rather than engaging in a discussion about how she should have avoided getting pregnant, she explained how she organized other teen mothers and forced the district to keep the child-care center open:

> They said that there were not enough girls to keep the center open, but I know that all my friends who have children would go to school if they could get child care. So I just called them and told them that they could graduate and get free child care. We had a meeting at my house, about 12 of us. I knew the superintendent of the district was coming to my school. The next week, I told my friends that we were going to confront the superintendent so that he would keep the child-care center open. How is he going to support education but won't let us graduate! So the next week when he came into the school with all the press and cameras, me and all my friends met him at the front door with all our crying children. I handed him Kiya [her baby] and said, "If you don't reopen this center, then maybe you can watch our children when we go to school and get an education." Well, the next day, I was informed that the district was going to keep the center open.

Lateefa's ethnic identity and political consciousness reframed her personal issue. Instead of being a powerless black and pregnant teen statistic she was an active community member with the capacity to challenge the school district to meet her needs as a new mother. Ultimately, as a result of the center reopening, Lateefa graduated from high school and through working with Leadership Excellence staff was admitted to San Jose State University. During her 1st year of college she struggled with raising her daughter and completing schoolwork. Despite these challenges, she founded her own student-run organization to support college students with children. She organized other young women on campus who she knew struggled with the same issues she dealt with, such as child care; rent subsidies; and, more important, isolation from other students, who enjoyed their free time and parties without the demands of raising a child. Lateefa elaborated:

> We would meet on Thursday afternoons with our children after class in the student union. It was cool because we could just talk about our children and discuss issues we believed were important to mothers. After the first couple of sessions we realized that we were all dealing with similar issues so we began to organize around what we thought was most important.

Activism for Lateefa involved more than skills and knowledge about how to organize; it involved a racial consciousness about her capacity to change circumstances she viewed as unjust. Her racial identity served as a catalyst, impelling her to act on behalf of others who shared similar experiences both as African Americans and as parents. Her activism was directed inward, by her embracing her identity, then outward, by her acting on behalf of those who shared similar identity-based struggles.

Similar to Lateefa, Tre became involved with pressing community issues in Oakland. His return to Oakland, however, was not easy, because he needed time to readjust to urban life and deal with his friends, who didn't understand the changes in his attitude, appearance, and identity. Tre described returning to Oakland:

> When I came back to Oakland I stayed in the house a lot because I had to learn how to adapt back to this society. I had gotten used to letting my guard down in Ghana, and not watching over my back. I actually didn't feel threatened so I just let my guard down. I remember in Ghana I went to a club where a bunch of black men were hanging out. I was kinda nervous because I was thinking if a bunch of blacks get together then somebody is about to get shot. I was standing in the background, just watching, and then a bunch of brothers walked by and said to me, "How you doing, my brother," greeting me, and speaking to me. It just gave me an experience that I needed to see because I understand how blacks are supposed to be. That feeling is still with me. That feeling is like my hope, it lets me know that there's hope out here, you know?

He realized how the conditions in Oakland, rather than the young people, threatened the types of communal living and relationships he had seen in Ghana. He also became more conscious of how political, economic, and social conditions constrain Africans' lives in both Ghana and Oakland. His awareness also spawned a sense of responsibility to confront injustice in Oakland. Tre reflected on his sense of responsibility to act on behalf of other youth in Oakland:

> I'm fresh out of East Oakland and most people see me as one of the black youth you would expect to get killed or go to jail. But I went to Africa! I got a chance to experience that fresh off the streets. Being through hell in the streets and then going to Africa was shocking to me. I wish all my partners could have seen what I seen. It was a beautiful experience! But they didn't, so I have to take what I learned back to them, fight for what is missing in their lives.

Tre's commitment to fighting for social justice in his community was tested in early 2000. California governor Pete Wilson had placed on the ballot the Juvenile Justice Crime Bill, which would give prosecutors the power to send many juvenile cases to adult court. The measure proposed changes to laws specifically related to the treatment of juvenile offenders and changed laws for juveniles and adults who were suspected gang members. Specifically, the measure required more juvenile offenders to be tried in adult court and increased penalties for gang-related crimes. Tre first learned of the proposed bill during a political education meeting at the Leadership Excellence center. Having spent time in juvenile hall, and hearing the horror stories from his brother who had been incarcerated, Tre became involved with various efforts to defeat Proposition 21. After participating in rallies, marches, and numerous organizing meetings sponsored by local community-based organizations, he realized that although African American youth in Oakland would bear the brunt of disproportionate incarceration, he saw few African American youth involved with the organizing efforts. Many of the groups were multiracial coalitions of young people where no one ethnic group composed the majority. Tre viewed the lack of African American youth involvement in the organizing efforts as a failure on the part of many of the groups to attract and train black youth from Oakland:

> They are doing a good job at getting the youth involved but none of my friends have ever heard about Proposition 21 and don't really care. So I am doing all this political education on my own.

Tre's experience in Ghana had fostered a sense of collective responsibility and commitment to confronting racial injustice. Many of the events and political education opportunities occurred in the offices of several community-based organizations and rarely involved going to the parks, street corners, and barbershops where he knew many of his friends would congregate during the day. As a result, Tre initiated his own strategy to get more African American youth involved with the organizing efforts. He organized a series of political education session using "Guerilla hip-hop"— impromptu, mobile political concerts with music, rapping, and political education in local parks, in strip malls, and on street corners where young people hang out.

On his own initiative, he organized a group of about 15 youth from Leadership Excellence and recruited Boots Riley, leader of the political rap group The Coup, in order to get into the community and educate and organize black youth about the Juvenile Justice Crime Bill. Early one Saturday morning they rented a large flatbed truck and loaded it with a large PA system, turntables, microphones, and speakers. They met Boots and planned to drive to neighborhoods in Oakland that some organizers had avoided. With loudspeakers, a DJ, music, and Boots as a main attraction, they distributed thousands of fliers and spoke to hundreds of youth who would be most affected by this legislation. They held miniconcerts that lasted from 30 minutes to an hour in the parking lot of Eastmont Shopping Center and at Foothill Square. They stopped at local barbershops to distribute fliers and talk to black youth about the legislation. Through hip-hop, they were able to communicate the urgency of their political participation and begin building a base of support from black youth themselves.

Tre's participation in efforts to defeat Proposition 21 is an example of the relationship between identity development and transformative resistance. Tre's identity as an African American male was connected to the economic struggles experienced by his African peers in Ghana as well as the daily struggle he and his peers navigated on the streets of Oakland. His identity fostered a sense of civic responsibility to challenge and resist policies and issues he viewed as unjust and to create new pathways for political and civic engagement for other black youth in Oakland. Ultimately, Tre became more deeply involved with the "No on 21 Campaign" and participated in a series of actions that further developed his political consciousness. In February 2000, Tre joined hundreds of other young people in the San Francisco Bay Area who held marches and rallies, as well as picketed and occupied the headquarters of major corporate sponsors of Proposition 21. On February 19, Tre participated in "Get on the Bus!" guerilla street theater where youth boarded city buses and performed poems and short skits in order to provide political education and distribute fliers with information about the initiative. Despite these efforts, the California voters approved the proposition on March 7. Outraged by the passage of the proposition, nearly 400 youth flooded the lobby of the San Francisco

Hilton Towers Hotel, one of the largest corporate supporters of the legislation, chanting slogans, carrying signs, and staging a peaceful sit-in (Aguila, 2000). Tre commented on his experience with direct action:

> It was tight when we all came together to protest the Hilton. Like 400 of us marching toward the hotel all of a sudden became dead silent, then we busted into the lobby chanting. Police was taking people away but we just kept on coming into the lobby. I felt like I was part of something powerful and I think for the first time I started to see myself as an activist. You know, fighting for black people even though you might get arrested or something.

For Tre, identity served as a pathway to political action and opened up a new worldview about social issues that affect black youth. The trip to Africa laid the foundation for a strong racial identity and fostered new sense of collective responsibility and engagement. He stated:

> It was an amazing experience. For me it all started by me going to Africa because I feel like going there filled a lot of blanks that was missing in my life. Going to Ghana and then all this organizing was a real eye-opener because I think more critically about things that's going down. Like I learned in these political education sessions that you gotta get deeper into the root causes of things to see the truth. So basically going to Africa filled in the blanks for me because I got Mexican friends, they got they own little culture; my Asian friends, they got they language; and I'm like, I'm just black with no language so I ain't got shit. So I went to Africa, it made me feel like I got a culture. Like I remember when I would see a cat in the streets with a lot of jewelry on and he just walking, flossing, and something would trigger off in my head. I wanted to just go over kick his ass and take all of his shit. But now I didn't realize where that hate came from. It came from me hating myself! Now I see a person flossing, I might think that's a king right there and I respect him. I am more humble now and I have better way of thinking. Basically, I was asleep and now I am awake. I learned how to see Oakland differently now, and work with folks to make things better for black folks.

Identity development in Tre's case seems to be more than simply having a positive view of himself as African American; his identity came to provide life-affirming meaning where he cast away self-defeating behavior and engaged in forms of resistance that both celebrated black life and carved a pathway for justice in his community. Radical healing for Tre occurred by his reconstituting an identity that maintains an authentic connection to the realities of black urban life, but also is connected to a diasporic experience of struggle. This conceptualization of identity is a radical departure from Afrocentric discourse, which often promotes a static view of African identity rooted in ancient Egypt. Radical healing embraces a more dynamic understanding of identity that connects the transformation of the soul to the everyday lived realities of the streets. For both Lateefa and Tre, there wasn't a tension to reject their own black urban sensibilities and replace it with an African-centered identity. Instead, both identities existed side by side, which afforded a unique opportunity to both reflect and act in ways that refined, clarified, and connected their identity to social justice.

IDENTITY AND ACTIVISM

Identity promotes thriving rather than simply surviving in urban environments. Debates about the relationship between identity and activism have prompted researchers to examine how identity contributes to or inhibits various forms of social action (Cohen, 1985; Melucci, 1988). For African American youth whose identities are often distorted in the media, marginalized in school, and stigmatized in public policy, the capacity to resist toxic perceptions of black identity is central to the radical healing process. This means that the healing process must build an identity that is connected to a broader struggle for justice and is actively engaged in social change.

Identity development for black youth, in this sense, is not simply an individual process, but involves a collective exchange of ideas, symbols, and meanings that protect, defend, and reestablish the social category of black youth. For example, hip-hop culture has been used as a politicizing tool to inform youth about significant social problems (Kelley, 1996; Rose, 1994). Since the mid-1980s, groups such as Public Enemy seized the attention of many urban youth of color because of their ability to boldly criticize and reveal serious contradictions in American democracy. Rap artists such as Chuck D, KRS1, and Arrested Development called for youth to raise their consciousness about American society and become more critical about the conditions of poverty. Hip-hop groups such as Dead Prez, the Coup, and the Roots today provide black youth with an analysis of racism, poverty, sexism, and other forms of oppression. For many black youth, hip-hop culture is a vehicle for radical healing because it provides a space in which to express pain, anger, and the frustration of oppression.

The challenge for those of us who work with black youth is to acknowledge the struggles, victories, and defeats in black youths' lives without romanticizing resistance while simultaneously paying careful attention to agency. Somewhere between resistance and hopelessness lies the reality of the day-to-day struggles youth must navigate. Through a richer under-standing of identity and the healing process, we can conceptualize other important forms of political behavior that can be found as black youth re-discover their African roots in order to make their communities a better place.

6

An Emancipatory Vision for Black Youth: Toward an Ecologically Responsive Strategy for Justice

One of the great problems of history is that the concepts of love and power have usually been contrasted as opposites—polar opposites—so that love is identified with a resignation of power, and power with a denial of love. . . . What is needed is a realization that power without love is reckless and abusive, and love without power is sentimental and anemic. Power at its best is love implementing the demands of justice, and justice at its best is power correcting everything that stands against love.

Dr. Martin Luther King Jr., Presidential Address, Southern Christian Leadership Conference, 1967

THROUGHOUT THIS BOOK, I have argued for building the capacity of black youth to challenge injustice in their communities. The radical healing process is one way to build the capacity of youth to act to resist social marginalization and confront inequality in their communities. Through caring relationships, community connections, political consciousness, and cultural identity, black youth reengage in civic life by addressing issues that are closely connected to struggles in their everyday life. Rather than focusing on how urban decay and poverty foster delinquent and pathological behaviors among black youth, I illustrate how radical healing can prepare these young people to respond to such forces in ways that contribute to new, vibrant forms of civic life.

The 1960s and 1970s black radical activism has given way to new forms of activism in the black community. These modes of activism involve rebuilding hope and healing from years of oppressive social, economic, and educational conditions. The healing process fosters a vision for social change and a passion for justice. There are many organizations that under-stand that healing is a critical component of post–civil rights activism in black communities. Building upon the legacy of 1960s civil rights orga-nizations, black activist organizations today focus on building activism among black youth through hip-hop culture, poetry, and film. Perhaps what is most powerful about these modes of activism is that they all have created a vision of how black communities can heal, organize, and build new spaces of possibilities.

The Malcolm X Grassroots Movement, for example, is an organization of black artists, activists, and organizers who work collectively to defend the human rights of African American people. Through an analysis of white supremacy and structural racism, the organization educates, organizes, and politicizes black communities. This new generation of black activists ar-gues that building community control and self-determination are critical to challenging racial oppression in black communities. With chapters in Oakland, California; Washington, DC; Atlanta, Georgia; and Jackson, Mis-sissippi, the Malcolm X Grassroots Movement has sparked a new vision of black radicalism.

Through Black August, the commemoration of the assassination of political prisoner George Jackson in August 1971, the Malcolm X Grassroots Movement builds new forms of black youth activism. Using hip-hop as a cultural catalyst to bring young people together, Black August showcases progressive hip-hop artists and provides international exchanges for ac-tivists. These activities provide young people with political education and the capacity to mobilize thousands of young people. On September 20, 2007, the Malcolm X Grassroots Movement helped to mobilize nearly 20,000 activists to go to Jena, Louisiana, to protest the unfair court decision to try six black males with attempted second-degree murder while their white victim was barely injured in a high school fight.

The radical healing process is also evident in their work. There are clearly marked pathways for caring relationships with youth, well-established community connection, opportunities for political education, and rich exposure to African culture. The Malcolm X Grassroots Movement is just one example of contemporary activism among young black adults. Most significant about organizations similar to the Malcolm X Grassroots Move-ment is the clear emancipatory vision for black youth and their unwavering commitment to freedom. For example, organizations such as Brotherhood Sister Soul in New York provide opportunities for Black and Latino youth to create a new vision for their communities and their own lives. Based in Harlem, the organization works with hundreds of youth by providing aca-demic skills, political consciousness, and social opportunities to envision the type of world they want to create. Similarly, the 21st Century Youth

Leadership Movement in Selma, Alabama, works with black youth to inspire, assist, organize, and develop the leadership skills necessary to confront 21st-century challenges in black communities. Building from lessons
from the civil rights movement, the 21st Century Youth Leadership trains
young black people to use their leadership to create a just society.

Small grassroots organizations such as these represent new forms of
activism in the context of black urban communities. Often these organizations foster among young people shared interests, collective identities,
mutual trust, and the capacity to act on behalf of the common good.
Through the radical healing process, these organizations create opportunities for youth to imagine, hope, dream, and create new possibilities for
their communities and our society. These opportunities are critically important, given the preponderance of youth programs and services in urban
black communities that focus almost entirely on preventing problems rather
than creating opportunities for social action. For many of us working in
education, youth development, and community-based organizations, positive change is often viewed as "fixing" black youth. The very structure of
funding often requires that we reduce youth violence, increase academic
performance, or prepare youth for employment. The emphasis on programs
that exclusively focus on harm reduction or prevention simply is not
enough. Problem negation is not a social justice approach. Social justice
educators and teachers must learn to connect resistance with creating, organizing with dreaming, and activism with hope. Making these connections provides us with a more holistic and richer understanding of what
constitutes social justice. More attention is needed to understand those
factors that encourage and support social action among African American
youth. Makani Themba accurately points out that prevention and harm
reduction, while important, presume that young people simply don't know
any better. Numerous fliers encouraging youth to stop smoking, end violence, or go to school do little to address these issues. She argues that, con-
trary to conventional wisdom, information is not power. "Rather power is
the capacity to make changes and choices and to be heard; and to define,
control and defend and promote one's interests" (1999, p. 21). Many of the
problems facing black youth come from lack of power, not lack of information. The capacity for youth, for example, to sit on police review boards
and participate in hiring teachers and school principals focuses more on
shifting power to young people than on fixing behavior. The key to change
is creating the space for young people to imagine a better way of life and
support them so they can act on that vision.

Black youth today, as they did in the past, grow up with a passion for
justice. However, in urban communities such as Oakland, poverty, joblessness, and violence have not only taken a toll on urban life, but also threat-

ened the capacity for black youth to hope and dream of justice in their communities. Police harassment, poor schools, and unresponsiveness to violence are constant reminders of injustice in their everyday lives. While black youth are very much aware of injustice in their lives, there are few opportunities for them to nurture and develop a social justice consciousness. In Oakland, for example, the destruction of the Black Panther Party, combined with few opportunities for viable employment and the spread of crack cocaine, all contributed to the decline of important forms of organizational and civic life. This decline has limited the opportunities for young people to build their capacity to fight for social justice.

All this illustrates how urban environments shape the content and form of civic life for black youth. Through a detailed examination of the Leadership Excellence programs and practices in Oakland, I have described how radical healing encourages reflection on personal issues and social conditions in order to develop political awareness and social action. This strategy provides insight into an *ecologically responsive* approach to working with black youth. An ecologically responsive approach simply means building the capacity of young people to act upon their environment in ways that contribute to well-being for the common good. Learning becomes richer and more meaningful when young people intervene in issues that shape their daily lives.

Radical healing as an ecologically responsive strategy highlights (1) the socially toxic conditions in urban communities, (2) the process for building the capacity for youth to respond to these conditions, and (3) the ways in which social justice, agency, and resistance can contribute to individual, community, and broader social wellness. Young people recognize how this process contributes to their own sense of well-being, as well as community and social wellness. A former Leadership Excellence participant commented:

> I can tell you one thing about Leadership Excellence is that it will spark you to act. Honestly, Malcolm X was the pimp and the hustler, but when he got turned on to some knowledge about his self, his community, and his history it changed his life. Look what he did, he became a leader and influenced many people. So they feed me tablespoon after spoon all this knowledge, about myself, black empowerment. After a while, I began to be hungry for what they were feeding me. So even if you were to change one person with Leadership Excellence, we never know how that opportunity will impact the world.

An ecologically responsive strategy has several policy implications. Leadership Excellence, in many ways, has served as an incubator of innovation for working with black youth. Typically, small grassroots community organizations can experiment, implementing new strategies under the radar of school policies and governmental regulations that restrict the type of work that black youth need. Policy advocates must have the courage to bring to the center unconventional strategies that inspire young people to act. A former Leadership Excellence participant stated:

> We get so empowered with the programs, but it's up to us to keep it going. Programs like that should also be schools, because of the impact that they have on us. It really takes programs like this to make a difference. But it will take people in city and state government, you know, to really recognize the power of these little organizations. Community organizations need support so that they could build and begin to do some of the things that everyone knows should be done. It will take these type of community organizations who are dedicated, who have what it takes to stir people up again. It is really important for my friends to have the type of experience that I have had. So I am working to pass on what I gained to my community, and keep it going.

Sustaining this type of community work will require both policy advocates and practitioners who recognize the importance of healing and social action.

RADICAL HEALING IN POLICY AND PRACTICE

What does radical healing mean for public policy? How can educators and youth workers use a radical healing process? What practices can reshape how we work with black youth? Policy makers, educators, and youth workers must not simply consider short-term strategies that focus on preventing problems among black youth, but instead embrace a long-term emancipatory vision that supports civic and political engagement among black youth. I believe that an emancipatory vision for black youth involves three ideas.

Articulate a Clear Vision About the Society in Which We Live

First, we must be able to articulate a clear vision about the society in which we live. Rather than concentrating on what behaviors we want to eliminate or reduce among black youth, we need to focus on what type of world we want to see. This might mean envisioning a society with racial and gender equality or imagining a community with a vibrant economy. The key is we must have a vision of our society in order to articulate a vision for youth. Both visions are inextricably linked together.

I have often discussed this idea with youth outreach workers or teachers who struggle with classroom discipline. I ask them, "Is the reduction of violence the same as creating peace? Or if our work was 100% successful in reducing or ending violence, would that constitute peace?" Similarly, I have asked youth development professionals, who sometimes have an unclear vision of what constitutes a productive healthy adult, "What are we developing our youth to become?" My experience has been that we have been so constrained by our focus on reduction of problems that we have lost our ability to create new programs and strategies. Those who struggle with these questions have rarely considered what peace looks like other than the absence of violence.

Articulating our vision for black youth not only provides clear direction, but also is inspiring, life affirming, and uplifting. Our capacity to create is more powerful than our ability to destroy. Activists in the 1960s clearly understood that the pursuit of a worthy vision is as important as achieving the goal itself. Perhaps just as important as the political organizing during the 1960s was a common vision for equality and justice. The collective goal was not simply to end segregation; they sought to create a just society. Black youth endured the brutal violence that resulted from sitting in at lunch counters in Greensboro, North Carolina, or marching in Selma, Alabama, because of a commitment to common vision for our society.

If we listen closely, we can hear the ways in which black youth articulate a new vision for our society. Conversations among black youth in barbershops, in parks, and on street corners not only highlight how things are, but also how things should be. Themba (1999) reminds us that oppressed communities have conversations out of view from the mainstream society about how the world should be. For oppressed communities these conversations often validate what people feel and experience every day and create a collective consciousness about how things should be. Robin Kelly explores the role of black radical imagination in black social movements throughout history. He suggests that:

> progressive social movements do not simply produce statistics and narratives of oppression; rather, the best ones do what great poetry always does: transport us to another place, compel us to relive horrors, and more importantly, enable us to imagine a new society. We must remember that the conditions and the very existence of social movements enable participants to imagine something different, to realize that things need not always be this way. (2002, p. 9)

One place to learn how black youth envision social change is through hip-hop culture. Although some of hip-hop culture is commercialized, contradictory, and sometimes even retrograde, we can learn how black youth envision society. In order to learn about this vision, however, we have to look beyond music lyrics and videos. Jeff Chang (2005) chronicled how New York City's economic decline and the layoffs in the public schools during the 1970s gave rise to hip hop. In response to years of gross disinvestment in New York's low-income communities, youth formed networks of break-dance clubs, DJ crews, and neighborhood hip-hop block parties that encouraged youth from neighborhoods that were once at war with each other to come together and compete through dancing or rapping. This ultimately served to mitigate violence in the Bronx and provided limited economic opportunities for local hip-hop artists. Similarly, Sullivan (1997) argued that in the absence of traditional participatory opportunities such as student government, community review boards, and youth volunteering, some black youth participate in an intricate network of relationships between hip-hop artists, party promoters, filmmakers, and youthful hip-hop clubs that provide black youth with tangible organizing skills. More recently, Kitwana (2002) discussed how the proliferation of new hip-hop political organizations such as Hip-Hop Summit Action Network (HSAN) or the National Hip Hop Political Convention in 2004 sought to garner the resources and energy of the hip-hop generation in order to build a common political platform relevant to the needs of millions of disenfranchised youth and young adults.

These efforts point to the ways in which black youth articulate a political vision for the communities in which they live. Hip-hop culture is forging a new paradigm with which to conceptualize social organization among black youth in urban America. Through music and culture, black youth and young people throughout the country are increasingly frustrated by the inability of after-school programs and social services to confront the oppressive conditions in urban communities.

Our vision for African American youth must view educational success and academic achievement as a way to create a more just world. Embracing an emancipatory vision for youth means that academic outcomes are tools used to achieve justice. This vision also resonates with young people who feel the brunt of social inequality in their daily lives and often question the purpose of academic success. Youth who struggle to work and go to school, attend underfunded schools, and experience teachers who don't care find little meaning in school when it is not connected to their everyday lives. Youth are more engaged in school when they are exposed to ideas that raise their consciousness about social inequality and builds their capacity to change it. Research supports this idea. In their study of six grassroots community-organizing efforts, the Community Involvement Program of the Annenberg Institute found that organizing contributed to increased student attendance, improved test scores, and higher graduation rates and college-going aspirations (Mediratta et al., 2008).

Prepare African American Youth to Confront Power Inequality in Their Schools, Communities, and Society

African American youth are not passive victims of social neglect. Rather, many find remarkable ways to struggle collectively to improve the quality of their lives. Therefore, the second component of an emancipatory vision for African American youth is to prepare African American youth to confront power inequality in their schools, communities, and society. For educators, youth workers, and policy advocates this means shifting from a "fixing" perspective to an "action" perspective. This simply means that we must consider how structural inequality shapes young people's lives while at the same time prepare youth to contest, challenge, respond, and negotiate the use and misuse of power.

Despite the tremendous challenges that young people experience in urban environments, with support and guidance, youth can respond in ways that support their development and contribute to a vibrant community life. The action perspective requires that youth understand how the misuse of power in institutions such as their schools make their lives more difficult. For example, in providing youth with a power analysis of their school, one might ask youth, "Who has the power to influence the quality of your education?" Such analysis of power often reveals hidden systems of privilege that encourage critical thinking about social problems.

Preparing youth to confront power inequality develops their capacity to address school and community issues that do not meet their needs. This process rejects blaming young people for school and community problems. Rather, young people strategize, research, and act to change school policies, state legislation, and police protocols that create and sustain inequality. Systemic change focuses on root causes of social problems and makes explicit the complex ways that various forms of oppression work together. This helps counter the low self-esteem that comes from youth being blamed for their own oppression.

Some reading this may be apprehensive about training youth activists. Others might have concerns that preparing African American youth to organize could further exacerbate tensions with adults who already view black youth as civic and social "problems." In response to these concerns, I am reminded of an essay by Audre Lorde, who suggested that silence is never a substitute for action. Educators, policy advocates, and youth workers must acknowledge the purpose of action, and sometimes righteous anger, in social change activities. Lorde suggested that anger must be expressed if it is to be a tool for social change. "Anger is loaded with information and energy. . . . Properly focused and translated into action in the service of our vision, it can become a powerful source of energy serving progress and change" (1995, p. 127). Lorde's comments suggest that anger has an important role in social change efforts. Her comments represent a convergence of mental health and civic life and are strikingly similar to those of Janie Ward (2000), who argued that parents who successfully instill healthy psychological resistance in their children help them cope with, rather than repress, anger and frustration. This is essential to building psychological health among African American youth.

Action in response to injustice can contribute to well-being and mental health among African American youth. While this is not a new idea, it does open some interesting opportunities for further research in this area. Watts and Guessous (2006) offer a sociopsychological discussion about the sociopolitical development of youth and the role of social oppression. Their study surveyed 131 youth about their capacity to change things they believed to be unfair. They found that black youth who displayed a strong belief that they could change things also displayed higher levels of mental health and youth development outcomes.

Developing an action perspective involves teaching and learning about the root and systemic causes and effects of a particular community or social problem. It entails transforming a problem into an issue and identifying parties responsible for bringing about desired changes. The action perspective also builds important cognitive skills that allow youth to develop meaningful and innovative solutions to school and community issues. In addition to critical thinking, relationship building, and identity development, the action perspective makes youth issues more central to overall community change efforts. This process broadens young people's understanding of power and how institutions affect their lives. For example, teachers working with students have developed surveys that include such questions as, "Did you have books in all your major subjects this year?" "Are you allowed to take books home?" "Where do you feel safe at your high school?" "What would you do to improve the lunchroom?"

After analyzing the surveys, youth may learn that safety is a primary concern at their school. This information could be used to build important analytical skills such as critical thinking, consensus and relationship building, and how to negotiate and compromise with and navigate bureaucratic institutions. It also involves recruiting allies and members and educating the general public about safety at school. Action involves a wide range of activities that include speaking at a city council meeting, informational picketing, writing letters, signing petitions, displaying banners, and having walkouts. Some forms of action, however, are more subtle. Building optimism, hope, and the belief that youth can change things is an important form of action and is also important political currency. More than simply creating a ruckus and getting media attention through organizing, action involves modeling the vision and living and treating each other with compassion and justice.

Action provides pathways for finding life purpose and experiences that can help shape their sociopolitical identities well into adulthood. Often such experiences translate to new worldviews about social issues where young people see their communities as a place of possibility and change. Miranda Yates and James Youniss (1998) found in their yearlong study that black youth who participated in civic or political activities developed a greater understanding of social justice and civic responsibility over time. Action connects the personal with the political because it removes self-blame and helps young people see the connections between personal life challenges and broader social issues.

Build a Purpose Through Identity and Culture

Perhaps one of the most significant aspects of an emancipatory vision for African American youth is fostering an African identity that is deeply committed to justice and freedom. This perspective embraces Africa as a cultural starting point for African peoples throughout the world and rejects white supremacist ideas about black identity. While I have argued elsewhere that there are limitations to some versions of African-centered education (Ginwright, 2004) some forms of African-centered pedagogy provide black youth a critical counternarrative of white supremacy and a strong sense of purpose and belonging. Culture alone is not an antidote to academic performance and social action, but is one important aspect of building a healthy identity. African-centered approaches that interrogate multiple forms of domination—class, gender, sexual orientation—must make the importance of justice more explicit in the identity-development process. This means that our understanding of African culture must be rooted in freedom, justice and liberation. Our understanding of culture must both free us from racist African images and avoid restrictive views of what constitutes African-centered identity. For African American youth, neither perspective captures the nuance, complexity, and authenticity of their everyday lives.

My point is that we should not reject African-centered approaches to working with black youth altogether. The paradigmatic shift toward African culture and philosophy is simply too valuable to discount. However,

we should continue to challenge, push, and develop African-centered schol-
arship and practice in ways that allow us to confront the crisis of black youth
today.

An emancipatory vision for black youth means that being rooted in
African culture is a starting point for identity development, but not the end
point. Our understanding of culture and identity development must be
viewed as a pathway to justice and freedom. First, this requires an acknowl-
edgment that African cultural identity is perhaps the most effective weapon
to fight white supremacy. For black youth who internalize negative images
of black people without knowing why, culture is a powerful vehicle to
uncover their hidden shame of being black. Once black youth understand
why blackness is degraded around the world, they can identify ways that
they degrade blackness in their own lives. They may question, for example,
why they enjoy "yo mama so black" jokes or why they find themselves more
attracted to lighter complexions. Cultural identity development must strive
to free young people's consciousness from damaging ideas about Africans
while at the same time reconstitute an identity that is healthy and whole.

Constant and relentless questioning of black youth's assumptions about
black identity can develop in them social justice habits. Social justice habits are routine and often mundane unconscious behaviors that over time
develop a critical collective consciousness. Social justice habits are important for black youth because these habits reveal hidden assumptions that
govern their language and identity. When black youth learn to question a
common phrase like "What's up, my nigga?" they can discover the word's
historical and contemporary implications.

Second, culture and identity provide black youth with purpose that is
both rooted in the history of black struggle and connected to problems in
everyday life. Murrell (1993) made this point by suggesting that Africans
in America viewed education and literacy as an act of freedom in post-
emancipation America. He suggests that

> Africans in America continue to struggle against institutionalized inequal-
> ity, which makes our heritage of literacy very different from that of the main-
> stream American culture. . . . Out of a history of disenfranchisement and
> denial of access to education, the Africanist cultural value emerged—literacy
> as the practice of emancipation. (pp. 30–31)

Murrell suggests that freedom, liberation, and justice are values rooted
in African culture and can guide and direct pedagogical practices. The
challenge is to build a cultural consciousness among black youth that can
interrogate issues in everyday life. To accomplish this, we must grapple
with questions such as how culture encourages black youth to confront
police brutality. How can African cultural identity encourage black youth

to organize in order to gain access to culturally appropriate books and school materials?

IN PURSUIT OF WHAT IT TAKES

Those of us who work closely with African American youth should constantly question and challenge approaches that cannot confront these difficult questions. However, it requires that we make difficult choices about our own lives. Effective work with African American youth requires more than simply step-by-step recipes for success. The conditions that black youth find themselves in did not come about from simple three-step recipes so we should not expect simple solutions to difficult problems. During a training of youth workers in San Francisco in October 2008, one of the youth workers commented to me that "working with youth is not simply a job, it is a lifestyle." I think there is remarkable truth to his comment. Effectively working with African American youth requires a commitment to justice and vision for freedom. No graduate course, training program, or book can adequately provide this type of commitment. However, if we commit ourselves to a relentless pursuit of love, peace, and justice, perhaps we can achieve a better quality of life for young people, ourselves, and our society.

Epilogue

ON JANUARY 1, 2009, many of us woke up with new hopes and aspirations for what the new year would bring. For some, there were new resolutions to be broken, for others there were promises to find better jobs or spend more time with the kids. For many of us in Oakland, however, our New Year's Day came in with news that a 22-year-old black man, while handcuffed, had been shot and killed by a transit police officer. Oscar Grant had just left his 4-year-old daughter and was on his way to work and decided to take the subway. Oscar and his friends were escorted off the train by BART police who were responding to a call that a fight had broken out on the train. The officers lined up Grant and his friends, handcuffed them, and forced them to lie face down on the cold concrete for all the passengers to see. Despite the fact that Grant complied with all the officer's requests, Officer Mehserle, a white officer, yanked the gun from his holster and pulled the trigger and shot Grant in the back in plain view of shocked passengers. The horrifying event was captured on video and was quickly disseminated over the Internet.

The incident left many people in Oakland stunned, but witnessing the actual police shooting on the news and over the Internet was more than people could take. To make matters worse, BART officials offered a weak statement to the community about investigating the incident. The lack of concern on the part of BART unleashed moral outrage in Oakland. BART officials, the mayor's office, and city officials would be unprepared for what would follow. On January 7, local organizers gathered at the Fruitvale BART station, where the shooting had occurred, to stage a protest in response to BART's slow response and lack of community concern. As the protesters began marching toward downtown, the march erupted into rioting and vandalism. Cars were overturned and burned, and small storefront shops had their windows shattered. The Coalition Against Police Executions (CAPE), a collection of community-based organizations, local trade unions, community organizers, and young people met to strategize to capture the momentum and energy for activism that had been unleashed. This event sparked perhaps the most significant movement of young people in Oakland since the 1960s.

One week later, on January 14, another rally held in downtown Oakland drew thousands of Oakland residents, many of them African American youth, who understood the importance of speaking out about police brutality. Mayor Dellums, surprised by the large number of participants, was asked by participants to come and speak to the angry crowd that was gathered on the steps of City Hall. When he emerged from his office, his words fell on deaf ears. Many of the young people wanted their frustration validated; they wanted him to "bring the heat" to BART officials. Many residents were unaware that the mayor was responsible for expediting the investigation and facilitating the murder charges that were being sought against the officer.

In many ways the moment represented a shift from protests from the civil rights generation, strategies that placed an emphasis on legislative and institutional access, to hip-hop generation protest that focuses more on institutional creation and personal transformation. In Oakland, there is a long history of police misconduct and police shooting mostly unarmed black male citizens. CAPE responded to this case in ways that highlighted how these incidents are toxic to community members and traumatic to residents. In their list of four demands, they stated:

1. We want the immediate arrest, indictment, and prosecution of BART police officer, Johannes Mehserle for the murder of Oscar Grant III.

We believe Oscar Grant III was maliciously murdered, robbed of his human and civil rights, and killed, in part, because of his race, class, youth, and dress which constitutes a classic case of racial profiling at best and at worst, a systemic BART philosophy of harassment, intimidation and violence as regards it patrons and citizens.

2. We want the release of the names and suspension of all the officers accompanying Officer Mehserle on January 1, 2009, at the Fruitvale BART shooting until a thorough and comprehensive investigation has taken place.

We believe that Officer Mehserle's actions were not a case of a "bad apple," but indicative of a particular mentality and culture within BART police in particular and law enforcement in general that views young, black males as suspects, criminals, and enemies.

3. We want a public review of BART history, police policy, strategy, and philosophy to assess whether (A). BART police are really needed and (B). If needed, whether or not they need guns.

We believe that the BART police force operates from policies and attitudes that are biased, militaristic, and racist and this philosophy is manifested in the actions and attitudes of its officers. Consequently, we recommend a citizen review of all such policies with the intent of creating a citizen review board to monitor excessive force, supervise implementation of diversity training and conduct an analysis on whether funds allocated for police might best be used differently.

4. We want BART, in the spirit of restorative justice, to make community restitution, in part, by funding community-based healing centers throughout the city for grief counseling, conflict resolution, and healing.

We believe that the murder of Oscar Grant III is the latest chapter and Oakland's version of police, intracommunity, terrorist and war violence that presently engulfs the planet. Only through concerted effort, understanding, and dedicated work and discipline can our city extricate itself from this madness. Institutions whose sole purpose is the healing of hearts (that have been wounded by violence) are needed throughout the world to show our communities, nation, and world that there is a better way.

The last demand is consistent with the findings that emerged from Mayor Dellum's Task Force on Youth Safety and Violence that was conducted a year prior to the Grant shooting. Almost a year was spent talking to youth in Oakland about what they would like to see in their communities. Recommendation number 17 in the mayor's report argues for the creation of community-based healing centers in the most economically depressed areas of the city. The recommendation outlines how the impact of violence, poverty, and lack of access to health care have been traumatic to young people in Oakland (Oakland Moving Forward, 2008).

The call for healing by Oakland's youth and adults marks a new era for activism in Oakland. These forms of activism call for personal restoration, health and wellness, and demands for institutional change and justice. When communities come together and focus on what it takes to thrive rather than simply survive, new approaches and strategies emerge. In Oakland, the call for both healing and justice have converged and perhaps have created a new way to consider activism in the post–civil rights United States.

Notes

Introduction

1. "Things Done Changed," from *Ready to Die*, Bad Boy Records (1994).
2. Robin Kelly makes this point related to the study of black communities. He argues that ethnographic work in black communities has reinforced the notion that there is a black monolithic community, and continues to have a fascination with studying pathology among the black urban poor.
3. Although rational choice theorists, such as Carol Stack and Catherine Eden, have challenged the social breakdown thesis by conceptualizing agency among the working poor, the thesis continues to have currency among social science and educational researchers.
4. For example, in the decade between 1985 and 1995 nearly 70% of all the articles in the leading youth and adolescent research journals focused on youth problems, pathology, or prevention primarily for African American and Latino youth (Ayman-Nolley & Taira, 2000).

Chapter 1

1. Ishmael Reed uses the term "blues city" in his book *Blues City: A Walk Through Oakland.*
2. The last name is fictitious to protect the identities of the informants.

Chapter 4

1. State Department of Justice Crime Statistics.

References

Aguila, J. (2000, March 9). 175 held after protest of youth crime initiative. *The San Francisco Examiner*, p. A-9.

Akom, A. A. (2006). The racial dimensions of social capital: Toward a new understanding of youth empowerment and community organizing in America's urban core. In S. Ginwright, P. Noguera, & J. Cammarota (Eds.), *Beyond resistance! Youth resistance and community change: New democratic possibilities for practice and policy for America's youth* (pp. 81–92). New York: Routledge.

Anderson, E. (1990). *Streetwise: Race, class, and change in an urban community*. Chicago: University of Chicago Press.

Anderson, E. (1999). *Code of the streets: Decency, violence, and the moral life of the inner city*. New York: W. W. Norton.

Ayman-Nolley, S., & Taira, L. L. (2000). Obsession with the dark side of adolescence: A decade of psychological studies. *Journal of Youth Studies, 3*(1), 35–48.

Brooks-Gunn, J., Duncan, G. J., Klebanov, P., & Sealand, N. (1993). Do neighborhoods influence child and adolescent development? *American Journal of Sociology, 99*(2), 353–395.

Brownstein, H. H. (1996). *The rise and fall of a violent crime wave: Crack cocaine and the construction of a social crime problem*. Monsey, NY: Criminal Justice Press, Willow Tree Press.

Brunson, R. K., & Miller, J. (2006). Young black men and urban policing in the United States. *British Journal of Criminology, 46*(4), 613–640.

Burt, C. (1993). Anatomy of Oakland homicides. *Oakland Tribune*, p. A-1.

Butts, J. (1999, October). *Youth violence: Perception versus reality*. Washington, DC: The Urban Institute.

California Department of Finance. (2005). *California statistical abstract: Federal revenues and expenditures in California fiscal years, 1970–1971 to 2003–2004*. Sacramento: California Department of Finance.

Chang, J. (2005). *Can't stop won't stop*. New York: St. Martin's Press.

City of San Diego. (2007). *San Diego historical crime rates per 1,000 population, 1950–2007*. San Diego: Police Department Crime Statistics.

Cohen, J. (1985). Strategy or identity: New theoretical paradigms and contemporary social movements. *Social Research, 52*(4), 663–716.

Dance, L. J. (2002). *Tough fronts: The impact of street culture on schooling*. New York: RoutledgeFalmer.

Drake, S. C., & Cayton, H. R. (1993). *Black metropolis: A study of Negro life in a Northern city*. Chicago: University of Chicago Press.

Du Bois, W. E. B. (1898). The study of the Negro problem. *Annals of the American Academy of Political and Social Science, 11*(January), 1–23.

Du Bois, W. E. B. (1899). *The Philadelphia Negro: A social study*. Philadelphia: University of Pennsylvania Press.

Fantasia, R. (1988). *Cultures of solidarity: Consciousness, action, and contemporary American workers*. Berkeley, CA: University of California Press.

Fine, M., Freudenberg, N., Payne, Y., Perkins, T., Smith, K., & Wanzer, K. (2003). Anything can happen with the police around: Urban youth evaluate strategies of surveillance in public places. *Journal of Social Issues, 59*(1), 141–158.

Fordham, S. (1996). *Blacked out: Dilemmas of race, identity, and success at Capitol High*. Chicago: University of Chicago Press.

Fox, J. A., & Zawitz, M. W. (2007). *Homicide trends in the United States*. Retrieved November 6, 2008, from http://www.ojp.usdoj.gov/bjs/homicide/race.htm

Freire, P. (1993). *Pedagogy of the oppressed*. New York: Continuum.

Fuchs, E., Shapiro, R., & Minnite, L. (2001). Social capital, political participation, and the urban community. In S. Seagert, P. Thompson, & M. Warren (Eds.), *Social capital in poor communities* (pp. 290–324). New York: Russell Sage.

Garbarino, J. (1995). *Raising children in a socially toxic environment*. San Francisco, CA: Jossey-Bass.

Garbarino, J., & Abramowitz, R. (1992). The ecology of human development. In *Children and families in the social environment* (2nd ed.). New York: Aldine de Gruyter.

Ginwright, S. (2004). *Black in school: Afrocentric reform, urban youth, and the promise of hip-hop culture*. New York: Teachers College Press.

Ginwright, S. (2007). Black youth activism and the role of critical social capital in black community organizations. *American Behavioral Scientist, 51*(3), 403–418.

Ginwright, S., & Cammarota, J. (2007). Youth activism in the urban community: Learning critical civic praxis within community organizations. *International Journal of Qualitative Studies in Education, 20*(6), 693–710.

Ginwright, S., Noguera, P., & Cammarota, J. (Eds.). (2006). *Beyond resistance! Youth resistance and community change: New democratic possibilities for practice and policy for America's youth*. New York: Routledge.

Gregory, R. (1998). *Black corona: Race and the politics of place in an urban community*. Princeton: Princeton University Press.

Hilliard, D., & Cole, L. (1993). *The other side of glory: The Autobiography of David Hilliard and the Story of the Black Panther Party*. Boston: Little, Brown.

Hilliard, D., & Weise, D. (2002). *The Huey P. Newton reader*. New York: Seven Stories Press.

hooks, b. (1993). *Sisters of the yam: Black women and self-recovery*. Boston: South End Press.

hooks, b. (1995). *Killing rage: Ending racism*. New York: Henry Holt.

Hutchinson, E. O. (1994). *The assassination of the black male image*. New York: Simon & Schuster.

Independent Sector. (2001). *The new nonprofit almanac in brief: Facts and figures on the independent sector, 2001*. Washington, DC: Author.

Johnson, J. A. (1995). Life after death: Critical pedagogy in an urban classroom. *Harvard Educational Review, 65*(2), 213–230.

Kelley, R. (1996). Kickin' reality, kickin' ballistics: Gangsta rap and postindustrial Los Angeles. In W. E. Perkins (Ed.), *Droppin' science: Critical essays on rap music and hip-hop culture* (pp. 117–158). Philadelphia: Temple University Press.

Kelly, R. (2002). *Freedom dreams: The Black radical imagination.* Boston: Beacon Press.

Kitwana, B. (2002). *The hip-hop generation: Young blacks and the crisis in African American culture.* New York: Basis Civitas Books.

Klandermans, B. (1984). Mobilization and participation. *American Sociological Review, 49,* 583–600.

Lawrence-Lightfoot, S. (1997). *The art and science of portraiture.* San Francisco: Jossey-Bass.

Lee, H. K. (2004, December 14). "Riders" lied, brutalized man, ex-rookie testifies: Whistle-blower says he feared losing job by coming forward. *San Francisco Chronicle,* p. B–5.

Lemke-Santangelo, G. (1997). *Deindustrialization, poverty.* Unpublished manuscript, University of California, Berkeley.

Littles, M., Bowers, R., & Gilmer, M. (2008). *Why we can't wait: A case for philanthropic action: Opportunities for improving the live outcomes of African American males.* New York: Ford Foundation.

Lorde, A. (1995). Age, race, class, and sex: Women redefining difference. In M. L. Anderson & P. H. Collins (Eds.), *Race, class, and gender: An anthology* (pp. 187–194). Belmont, CA: Wadsworth.

MacDonald, H. (2004, Oct 27). Complaints against Oakland police rise. *Oakland Tribune,* p. 1.

Males, M. (1996). *The scapegoat generation: America's war on adolescents.* Monroe, ME: Common Courage Press.

Males, M. (1999). *Framing youth: Ten myths about the next generation.* Monroe, ME: Common Courage Press.

Males, M., & Macallair, D. (2000). *The color of justice.* Washington, DC: Building Blocks for Youth.

Mattis, J. S. (1997). The spiritual well-being of African Americans: A preliminary analysis. *Journal of Prevention and Intervention in the Community: Special Issue, 16*(1–2), 103–120.

Mattis, J. S., & Jagers, R. J. (2001). A relational framework for the study of religiosity and spirituality in the lives of African Americans. *Journal of Community Psychology, 29*(5), 519–539.

Mediratta, K., Shah, S., McAlister, S., Fruchter, N., Mokhtar, C., & Lockwood, D. (2008). *Organized communities, stronger schools.* New York: Annenberg Institute for School Reform at Brown University.

Melucci, A. (1988). Getting involved: Identity and mobilization in social movements. In *International Social Movements Research* (Vol. 1, pp. 329–348). Greenwich, CT: JAI Press.

Mincy, R. (Ed.). (2006). *Black males left behind.* Washington, DC: Urban Institute Press.

Murrell, P. (1993). Afrocentric immersion: Academic and personal development of African American males in public schools. In T. Perry & J. W. Fraser (Eds.),

Freedom's plow; Teaching in the multicultural classroom (pp. 231–260). New York: Routledge.

Mutua, A. D. (2006). *Progressive black masculinities.* New York: Routledge.

National Center for Charitable Statistics. (2006). *Number of nonprofit organizations in California, 1996–2006.* Washington, DC: Author

Noguera, P. (2008). *The trouble with black boys: And other reflections on race, equity, and the future of public education.* San Francisco: Jossey-Bass.

Oakland Moving Forward. (2008). *Oakland Moving Forward community task force report.* Oakland, CA: City of Oakland.

Oakland Police Department. (2008). *Summary of Part 1 crime offenses, 1969–2007.* Retrieved September 7, 2008, from http://gismaps.oaklandnet.com/crimewatch/pdf/HistoricalData.htm

Obidah, J., Jackson-Minot, M., Monroe, C., & Williams, B. (2004). Crime and punishment: Moral dilemmas in the inner-city classroom. In V. Siddle Walker & J. R. Snarey (Eds.), *Race-ing moral formation: African American perspectives on care and justice* (pp. 111–129). New York: Teachers College Press.

Office of the City Administrator. (2005). *City of Oakland Citizens' Police Review Board 2005 annual report.* Oakland, CA: City of Oakland

Ogbu, J. (1990). Minority education in comparative perspective. *Journal of Negro Education, 59*(1), 45–57.

Pitts, S. (2006). *Black workers in the Bay Area: Employment trends and job quality: 1970–2000.* Berkeley, CA: Center for Labor Research and Education, University of California–Berkeley.

Piven, F., & Cloward, R. (1979). *Poor people's movements: Why they succeed, how they fail.* New York: Vintage.

Poe-Yamagata, E., & Jones, M. (2000). *And justice for some.* Washington, DC: National Council on Crime and Delinquency.

Portes, A. (1998). Social capital: Its origins and application to modern sociology. *American Sociological Review, 24,* 1–24.

Poussaint, A., & Alexander, A. (2000). *Lay my burden down: Unraveling suicide and the mental health crisis among African-Americans.* Boston: Beacon Press.

Powell, T. (2007, January 8). Perspectives: If not Oprah, then who? *Diverse Issues in Higher Education.* http://www.diverseeducation.com/artman/publish/article-6842.html

Prilleltensky, I. (2008). The role of power in wellness, oppression and liberation: The promise of psychopolitical validity. *Journal of Community Psychology, 36*(2), 116–136.

Prilleltensky, I., Nelson, G., & Pierson, L. (2001). The role of power and control in children's lives: An ecological analysis of pathways toward wellness, resilience, and problems. *Journal of Community and Applied Social Psychology, 11,* 143–158.

Putnam, R. D. (1993). The prosperous community: Social capital and community life. *The American Prospect* (Spring), 35–42.

Rhomberg, C. (2004). *No there there: Race, class, and political community in Oakland.* Berkeley: University of California Press.

Robinson, T., & Ward, J. V. (1992). A belief in self far greater than anyone's disbelief: Cultivating resistance among African American female adolescents. In C. Gilligan, A. G. Rogers, & D. L. Tolman (Eds.), *Women, girls and psychotherapy: Reframing resistance* (pp. 87–103). New York: Haworth Press.

Rose, T. (1994). *Black noise: Rap music and black culture in contemporary America.* Middletown, CT: Wesleyan University Press.

Saegert, S., Thompson, J. P., & Warren, M. (Eds.). (2001). *Social capital and poor communities.* New York: Russell Sage.

Sampson, R. (2001). Crime and public safety: Insights from community-level perspectives on social capital. In S. Saegert, P. Thompson, & M. Warren (Eds.), *Social capital in poor communities* (pp. 89–114). New York: Russell Sage.

Sampson, R. J., Morenoff, J. D., & Earls, F. (1999). Beyond social capital: Spatial dynamics of collective efficacy for children. *American Sociological Review, 64*(October), 633–660.

Sampson, R. J., & Raudenbush, S. W. (1999). Systematic social observation of public spaces: A new look at disorder in urban neighborhoods. *American Journal of Sociology, 105*(3), 603–651.

Sánchez-Jankowski, M. (1991). *Islands in the street: Gangs and American urban society.* Berkeley: University of California Press.

Sanchez-Jankowski, M. (2002). Minority youth and civic engagement: The impact of group relations. *Applied Developmental Science, 6*(4), 237–245.

Sánchez-Jankowski, M. (2008). *Cracks in the pavement: Social change and resilience in poor neighborhoods.* Berkeley: University of California Press.

Seale, B. (1970). *Seize the time: The story of the Black Panther Party and Huey P. Newton.* Baltimore: Black Classic Press.

Self, R. O. (2003). *American Babylon: Race and the struggle for postwar Oakland.* Princeton: Princeton University Press.

Smith, J. A. (2004). *On the Jericho Road: A memoir of racial justice, social action, and prophetic ministry.* Downers Grove, IL: InterVarsity Press.

Smith, S. S. (2007). *Lone pursuit: Distrust and defensive individualism among the black poor.* New York: Russell Sage Foundation.

Somé, M. P. (1999). *The healing wisdom of Africa.* New York: Penguin Putnam.

Stevens, J. W. (2002). *Smart and sassy: The strengths of inner-city black girls.* New York: Oxford University Press.

Sullivan, L. (1997). Hip-hop nation: The undeveloped social capital of black urban America. *National Civic Review, 86*(3), 235.

Sullivan, M. (1989). *Getting paid: Youth crime and work in the inner city.* Ithaca, NY: Cornell University Press.

Themba, M. N. (1999). *Making policy making change.* Oakland, CA: Chardon Press.

Thompson, A. (1995). Caring and colortalk: Childhood innocence in White and Black. In V. Siddle Walker & J. R. Snarey (Eds.), *Race-ing moral formation: African American perspectives on care and justice* (pp. 23–37). New York: Teachers College Press.

Wacquant, L. (1998). Negative social capital: State breakdown and social destitution in America's urban core. *Netherlands Journal of the Built Environment, 13*(1), 25–40.

Wacquant, L. (2001). The advent of the penal state is not destiny. *Social Justice*, *28*(3), 81–87.

Ward, J. V. (1995). Cultivating a morality of care in African American adolescents: A culture-based model of violence prevention. *Harvard Education Review* (Summer), 175–188.

Ward, J. V. (2000). Raising resisters: The role of truth telling in the psychological development of African American girls. In L. Weis & M. Fine (Eds.), *Construction sites: Excavating race, class, and gender among urban youth* (pp. 50–64). New York: Teachers College Press.

Washington, K. (2007). *Social environmental trauma threat among African American youth.* Unpublished paper, San Francisco State University.

Watts, R. J., & Guessous, O. (2006). Sociopolitical development: The missing link in research and policy on adolescents. In S. Ginwright, P. Noguera, & J. Cammarota (Eds.), *Beyond resistance! Youth resistance and community change: New democratic possibilities for practice and policy for America's youth* (pp. 59–80). New York: Routledge.

Watts, R. J., Williams, N. C., & Jagers, R. J. (2003). Sociopolitical development. *American Journal of Community Psychology, 31*(1/2), 185.

West, C. (1993). *Race matters.* Boston: Beacon Press.

Willis, P. (1977). *How working class kids get working class jobs.* Farnborough, UK: Saxon House.

Wilson, W. J. (1987). *The truly disadvantaged: The inner city, the underclass, and public policy.* Chicago: University of Chicago Press.

Wilson, W. J. (1996). *When work disappears.* New York: Random House.

Yates, M., & Youniss, J. (1998). Community service and political identity development in adolescence. *Journal of Social Issues, 54*(3), 493–512.

Young, A. (2004). *The minds of marginalized Black men: Making sense of mobility, opportunity, and future life chances.* Princeton: Princeton University Press.

Index

About the Author

SHAWN GINWRIGHT is an Associate Professor of Education in the Africana Studies Department and Senior Research Associate for the Cesar Chavez Institute for Public Policy at San Francisco State University. He is the founder of Leadership Excellence, Inc., an innovative youth development agency located in Oakland, California. He is the author of *Black in School: Afrocentric Reform, Youth, and the Promise of Hip-Hop Culture* and co-editor of *Beyond Resistance! Youth Resistance and Community Change: New Democratic Possibilities for Practice and Policy for America's Youth.* He is a highly sought speaker to national and international audiences.